For Edward

Contents

Note on the References and Acknowledgments   *ix*
Chronology: George Eliot's Life and Works   *xi*

LITERARY AND HISTORICAL CONTEXT

    1.   Historical Context   3
    2.   The Importance of the Work   9
    3.   Critical Reception   12

A READING

    4.   Preface: The Epigraph   23
    5.   Lantern Yard   28
    6.   Raveloe   45
    7.   The Red House   62
    8.   The Stone-pit   84
    9.   Epilogue: Part 2 of *Silas Marner*   106

Notes and References   117
Bibliography   121
Index   127

Note on References
and Acknowledgments

The text of *Silas Marner* for this study is that of the Penguin edition, edited by Q. D. Leavis (Harmondsworth, England, 1967); hereafter cited in text by page number only. References to other works by George Eliot are specified in the text. All page references are specified parenthetically in the text.

The chalk portrait of George Eliot used as a frontispiece is by Samuel Laurence and was drawn in 1860. It is reproduced with permission of the Mistress and Fellows of Girton College, Cambridge.

George Eliot, 1857 (1860?), Drawing in chalks by Samuel Laurence
The Mistress and Fellows, Girton College Cambridge

Chronology: George Eliot's Life and Works

1819	Mary Ann (or Marian) Evans born 22 November, the third of three children of Robert Evans, land agent for the estate of Arbury Hall near Nuneaton, Warwickshire. Christiana (Pearson) Evans, Mary Ann's mother, is Robert Evans's second wife, his first having died soon after the birth of her third child, which dies soon afterward. Mary Ann therefore has an elder stepbrother and stepsister, as well as an elder brother and sister. After her sister's death, her association with George Henry Lewes is to separate her from her brother Isaac, with whom she has enjoyed an especially close association since early childhood.
1828	Sent to Miss Wallington's Boarding School in Nuneaton, where she is strongly influenced by Maria Lewis and the evangelical movement within the Church of England.
1832	Attends the Misses Franklin's School in Coventry. Parliament passes the Great Reform Bill.
1836	Mother dies. Returns to keep house for her father. [First of Dickens's *Pickwick Papers* published.]
1841	Her father retires, and she moves with him to Foleshill, near Coventry, where she is drawn into the freethinking intellectual circle of Charles and Cara Bray and Charles Hennell.
1842	Refuses to attend church with her father, initiating four months' estrangement from him during which he comes close to turning her out of the house.
1843	[Thomas Carlyle's *Past and Present* published.]
1844	Translates David Strauss's *Das Leben Jesu* (*The Life of Jesus*), (published 1846).
1847	[Charlotte Brontë's *Jane Eyre* and Emily Brontë's *Wuthering Heights* published.]
1847–1848	[William Thackeray's *Vanity Fair* published.]
1849	Father dies. Travels with the Brays to Europe, staying for eight months in Geneva.

1850–1851   Meets John Chapman, editor of the *Westminster Review*. Becomes a contributor and moves to London, where she lives in a ménage à trois with Chapman and his wife, becomes assistant editor of the *Westminster*, and meets Herbert Spencer, for whom she entertains an unreciprocated affection.

1851–1853   [Mrs. Gaskell's *Cranford* published.]

1853   Meets George Henry Lewes, novelist, scientist, and historian of ideas, with whom she begins a liaison the following year. [Harriet Martineau's translation of Comte's *Cours de Philosophie Positive* published.]

1854   Eliot's translation of Ludwig Feuerbach's *Das Wesen des Christenthums* (*The Essence of Christianity*) published.

1855   [George Henry Lewes's *The Life and Work of Goethe* published. Anthony Trollope's *The Warden* published.]

1855–1856   Translates Spinoza's *Ethics* (never published) and writes two of her most celebrated essays for the *Westminster*: "The Natural History of German Life" and "Silly Novels by Lady Novelists." Writes "Amos Barton," the first of her *Scenes of Clerical Life*.

1857   "Amos Barton" published in *Blackwood's Magazine* under the pseudonym George Eliot. Writes "Mr. Gilfil's Love Story" and "Janet's Repentance," the second and third of *Scenes of Clerical Life*.

1858   *Scenes of Clerical Life* published.

1859   *Adam Bede* published. [Darwin's *The Origin of Species* published.]

1860   Accompanies Lewes on a month's stay in Italy. *The Mill on the Floss* published. Writes "Brother Jacob."

1861   *Silas Marner* published.

1863   *Romola* published.

1864   Travels with Lewes to Italy.

1865   Takes excursion to Paris and Brittany.

1866   *Felix Holt, the Radical* published. Travels with Lewes to Holland, Belgium, and Germany, and later to Spain.

1867   Parliament passes the Tory Parliamentary Reform Bill. Travels with Lewes to Germany.

1868   *The Spanish Gypsy* (poem) published. Travels with Lewes to Germany and Switzerland.

1868–1869   [Browning's poem *The Ring and the Book* published.]

1869   [J. S. Mill's *The Subjection of Women* published.] Travels with

Lewes to Italy. Meets John Walter Cross in Rome. Thornton Lewes, son of George Henry, dies.

1871–1872   *Middlemarch* published.

1872   [Hardy's *Under the Greenwood Tree* published.] Travels with Lewes to Germany.

1873   Travels with Lewes to France and Germany.

1874   *The Legend of Jubal* (poem) published. Travels with Lewes to France and Belgium.

1875   Bertie Lewes, another of Lewes's children, dies in South Africa.

1876   *Daniel Deronda* published. Travels with Lewes to France and Switzerland. [Henry James's *Roderick Hudson* published.]

1878   George Henry Lewes dies suddenly. George Eliot is prostrated with grief during the next few months.

1879   Publishes George Henry Lewes's *The Study of Psychology*. Completes and publishes his *Problems of Life and Mind*. John Blackwood, her publisher, dies.

1880   Marries her financial adviser, John Walter Cross, who is 40. On hearing of the marriage, her brother Isaac communicates with her for the first time since her association with Lewes began. Dies 22 December of heart failure following acute laryngitis.

LITERARY AND HISTORICAL CONTEXT

1

Historical Context

THE INTELLECTUAL CONTEXT

As well as being among the most intelligent of English novelists, George Eliot was the most intellectual of the novelists of her own day and of the preceding 150 years of novel writing. Henry Fielding and Walter Scott had been men of wide interests and broad intelligence, but their intelligence had been of a practical turn, and the play of ideas in their novels is not at all conspicuous. Thomas Love Peacock enjoyed playing with ideas, but the works of fiction he produced are scarcely novels at all, because the novelist's interest in character is so evidently subordinated to the pleasures of conversation and the discharge of genial satire. George Eliot's contemporaries—Wm. Thackeray, Anthony Trollope, Charles Dickens—often entertain strong political and social views, but they never give the impression that they have thought them through from first principles, and they rarely show us characters in their books engaged in the activity of intellectual reflection. George Eliot does all of these things. She was an intellectual before she was a novelist, and her writings include a great deal of what might be called popular philosophy and the history of ideas. Her novels are full of thinking people, caught up in the intellectual currents of the day. They offer accounts of these people's thinking that engage, and are meant to engage, the full intelligence of their readers.

The ideas she is concerned with are those that had been transmitted to the Victorian intelligentsia for the most part by the Romantic philosophers and poets of the late eighteenth and early nineteenth centuries. It was a European, not merely an English legacy, and included the poetry of Goethe, the drama of Schiller, the political theory of Rousseau, as well as the literature and philosophy of the native English tradition. Among her earliest publications is a translation of the German theologian David Strauss's *The Life of Jesus* and the philosopher Ludwig Feuerbach's *The Essence of Christianity*. Both translations appeared less than 15 years after the original publications in German, showing that at an early age George Eliot had far surpassed her *Middlemarch* Bible scholar Edward Casaubon's researches in the field of comparative religion. In the middle years of the nineteenth century, George Eliot traveled often and for long periods of time on the continent of Europe, especially in Germany, Switzerland, and Italy. In the last 15 years of her life she had acquired a European reputation and met on an equal footing such men as Franz Liszt, Richard Wagner, and the historian Theodor Mommsen. Even in the early 1850s, when she was coediting the *Westminster Review* with John Chapman, she was acquainted with emigré European thinkers such as the French socialist Louis Blanc and the Italian patriot Giuseppe Mazzini.

The *Westminster Review* gives a good indication of George Eliot's thought. It was founded in 1824 as the mouthpiece of philosophical radicalism and by the time it was bought by Chapman, in 1851, had become the principal forum of progressive thinking in England. It played the same sort of role in English intellectual and literary life as the *New Republic* played in America a hundred years later. Typical contributors were the historian J. A. Froude, the evolutionary scientist T. H. Huxley, the Utilitarian philosopher J. S. Mill, and the physicist John Tyndall. Huxley's mentor, Charles Darwin, had published *The Origin of Species* in 1859, two years before *Silas Marner*. In July and August 1858, George Eliot met Darwin's German translator, Victor

Carus, professor of comparative anatomy at Vienna. Her companion, George Henry Lewes, was a popular Darwinian and published his zoological observations on Darwin's new evolutionary theory, "Studies in Animal Life," in the *Cornhill Magazine* in 1860. George Eliot admired and was influenced by the thinking of these men. Her essays reveal her interest in political liberalism, the ethics of utilitarianism, and what she took to be the behavioral consequences of evolutionary theory. These interests are present in her novels, too, though there they coexist with a temperamental inclination to more conservative habits of thought. Many of her novels examine the mental conflict in people who are torn between old and new ways of thinking. These people may be intellectuals like Felix Holt, Tertius Lydgate, or Daniel Deronda, or they may be ordinary folk like Janet Dempster, Hetty Sorrel, and Maggie Tulliver, who find it difficult to articulate the conflict in their minds and hearts. On the whole the intellectuals tend to congregate in the later novels and the ordinary folk in the earlier ones.

Silas Marner was written in 1860–61, at the end of the first phase of George Eliot's writing. Nobody in it is much of a thinker, in the more elevated sense of the word. But many of its characters are given to general reflection, of however muddled a sort, on life and conduct. Dolly Winthrop and the villagers at the Rainbow might not be enormously gifted philosophers, but what sounds like the homespun wisdom or folly they give voice to often has its provenance in the books of the philosophers George Eliot had been reading.

THE LITERARY CONTEXT

On a first reading *Silas Marner* doesn't give the impression that it is written by an author of such formidable intellectual talents. Explicit literary references in the text tend to be to folk songs ("The Red Rovier" sung by Mr. Macey in chapter 6 or the tunes played by Solomon Macey) or to commonplace reading like Mant's Bible (an 1816 publication of the Authorized Version), which Nancy Lammeter is reading in chapter 17. Apart from the epigraph (from William Wordsworth's "Michael"), we have to wait until chapter 19 for the appearance of a quotation from a respected literary source, and that is again from Wordsworth—"beauty born of murmuring sound." It is so brief, and so similar in mood and diction to what surrounds it in George Eliot's prose, as to be effortlessly absorbed into the text. In her later novels, George Eliot got into the habit of attaching literary quotations (often of her own manufacture) to the opening of each of her chapters, but these too are absent from *Silas Marner*. Neither does she preface her chapters with those lengthy and often periphrastic titles ("Oliver [Twist] becomes better acquainted with the Characters of his new Associates; and purchases experience at a high Price. Being a short, but very important Chapter, in this History") that Fielding and Dickens include in their novels and that she herself contributes, in slimmed-down versions, to her own earlier work. It would be false to give the impression that *Silas Marner* looks as if it has been written by someone as naïf and unread as one of its own Raveloe villagers. Nevertheless, it is less heavily freighted with its author's intelligence even than such earlier examples of her work as *Adam Bede* and *The Mill on the Floss*.

Partly it is a simple matter of length. *Silas Marner* is a little less than 200 pages long. This is not much more than the story of Janet Dempster in "Janet's Repentance," the last of the three stories that constitute George Eliot's first work of fiction, *Scenes of Clerical Life*, and this was written deliberately as a story, not a novel. *Adam Bede* and *The Mill on the Floss* are each about three times as long, and all of the later novels are enormous. George Eliot wrote *Silas Marner* very rapidly, while she was meditating *Romola*—a vast, turgid, and almost unreadable historical novel set in fifteenth-century Florence—and immediately after completing another, shorter story about the theft of a hoard of golden guineas, called "Brother Jacob." She started it some time during the late summer of 1860, stalled for a while, and then wrote the bulk of it between the beginning of December and beginning of March 1861. Effectively, it took only four months to complete. This may account for the sense we have in reading it of a striking unity of purpose and clarity of theme. There are none of those loose ends, or misplaced subplots, or characters of equivocal status that disfigure so many otherwise grander and more ambitious Victorian novels. Everything is finished and to the point, so much so that in order to place *Silas Marner* in a tradition of writing we may have to go outside the mainstream of the history of the novel before the mid-nineteenth century to find analogues of this kind of fiction.

In an influential book, *The American Novel and Its Tradition*, Richard Chase[1] sets against the sane, equable, and prosaic characteristics of the English novel the wild and poetical character of the American romance. Novel and romance, he claims, were (and still are) the principal alternative forms available to the writer of fiction. The English excelled in the first, the Americans in the second. The English novel, he writes, "is notable for its great practical sanity, its powerful engrossing composition of wide ranges of experience into a moral centrality and equability of judgement" (Chase, 2). He argues that the English novel has included such "romantic" features as "oddity, distortion of personality, dislocations of normal life, recklessness of behaviour, malignancy of motive" (Chase, 2). But these are much more naturally attributed to the American romance, which reveals "an assumed freedom from the ordinary novelistic representation of verisimilitude, development and continuity; a tendency towards melodrama and idyl; a more or less formal abstractness and, on the other hand, a tendency to plunge into the underside of consciousness; a willingness to abandon moral questions or to ignore the spectacle of man in society, or to consider these things only individually or abstractly" (Chase, ix).

Reading *Middlemarch* and then *Moby Dick*, one sees what Chase means. These are the extreme cases that brilliantly illuminate the primary distinction. But there is a tradition of English writing that anticipates the American romance and shows its basic characteristics. It is a tradition that goes back at least as far as John Bunyan (*The Pilgrim's Progress*, 1678), including such fiction as Daniel Defoe's *Robinson Crusoe* (1719), James Hogg's *The Private Memoirs of a Justified Sinner* (1824), and, I would argue, Emily Brontë's *Wuthering Heights* (1847). The narratives often have an allegorical coloring. That is to say, the characters and situations that appear in them seem to have a representative, not primarily an individual, significance. As a result of this, the distribution of the events they record tends to produce a narrative displaying a marked degree of pattern, or explicit correspondence between one episode and another. *The Pilgrim's Progress* is a sort of parable in which the dream of Christian's journey from the City of Destruction to the Celestial City includes a great deal of parallel action, comparable scene and incident, explanations of the beliefs and experiences of the principal characters that point up clear similarities and differences. The same is true of the other narratives I have mentioned, and it is true also of such American romances as those of Nathaniel Hawthorne and Herman Melville.

Silas Marner has many of the same characteristics. The story of Silas can be described briefly in just such terms as Chase uses to describe the typical story of a romance: "oddity, distortion of personality, dislocation of normal life," etc. But while the principal subject and bold patterns of the story are romantic, the overall impression it makes on its readers is not. In the end, unlike *Wuthering Heights* for example, *Silas Marner* doesn't tell us anything about what is fundamentally mysterious in the human soul. Instead, it uses the matter and the manner of romance to produce a concentrated version of what we would expect to find in the novel as Chase defines it. That is why much of what follows places a great deal of stress on those aspects of *Silas Marner* that have most in common with the tale, the story, the romance. It then seeks to explain how George Eliot makes use of them to arrive at firm moral conclusions about human behavior that are very much the province of her own longer fictions. But the concentration and formal patterning that this sort of romance narrative displays entail subtle changes in the way those moral conclusions are drawn; and these, too, we look at in the detailed examination of the text that follows.

2

The Importance of the Work

For most of its length, *Silas Marner* is the most nearly perfect piece of writing George Eliot ever accomplished. The story of Silas's expulsion from the religious community of Lantern Yard, of his arrival at Raveloe and his accumulation there of his hoard of golden guineas, of the relationships of Godfrey and Dunstan Cass with the Squire, of Dunsey's theft of the guineas, and of the events occurring during the New Year's Eve dance at the Red House is consummately dealt with. The immediate consequences of the discovery of Molly Farren's body and of the baby are also convincingly described. The events of 16 years later, briefly related in Part 2, are less well handled; but this is a short section of seven, for the most part brief, chapters, and the main issue of the delayed judgment on Godfrey Cass and, indirectly, on his wife Nancy, is skillfully managed. None of George Eliot's other works of fiction is as good all the way through. Those sturdy narratives of guilt and repentance are always in danger of being undermined by a vein of unlovely high-mindedness or by lapses of control issuing from the author's sentimental self-identification with one or other of the dramatis personae.

The high-mindedness is everywhere apparent in George Eliot, but it is often matched by a subject seen to be genuinely worthy of it. Where this is the case there can be no objection. But sometimes the sense of worth is more apparent than real, and the presence of, say, Philip Wakem in *The Mill on the Floss* or of Will Ladislaw in *Middlemarch* goes some distance toward weakening what are otherwise in most respects admirable novels. Elsewhere the presence of these plaster saints is comprehensively baleful. The exhalation of old cassocks and the whiff of incense that attends them makes these characters unsympathetic to all but the most ardent of George Eliot's devotees. In his review of John Cross's *Life of George Eliot*, Henry James describes the Priory, where she lived from 1863 to 1880, as a "sequestered precinct."[1] He could remember well "a kind of sanctity in the place, an atmosphere of stillness and concentration, something that suggested a literary temple" (Carroll, 502). The few pictures of George Eliot that have come down to us are almost all pictures of the author of characters who might well be imagined as issuing from such a place. It is not a happy thought to be confronted by the subject of Sir Frederic Burton's chalk drawing of 1865, though it has to be added that such was that subject's personal magnetism that many of her contemporaries were happy to be so confronted. In later life she was herself made into the object of just such admiration as she had lavished on Romola and Deronda, with equally appalling results for her posthumous reputation. This did not recover until well into the present century (she died in 1880). For this reason I have chosen for the frontispiece of this book a less familiar chalk drawing by Samuel Laurence, which also has the attraction of having been sketched in 1860, at a date very close to that of the composition of *Silas Marner*.

The other fault, of indulgent self-identification with her characters, is present throughout the novels, but especially in the portrait of Maggie Tulliver in *The Mill on the Floss* and of Dorothea Brooke in *Middlemarch*. George Eliot's handling of these characters has been the subject of prolonged controversy in recent years, and there is no doubt that her perception of some of their faults is as intelligent as her emotional inclination to pardon them is overwhelming. But the one tends to be compromised by the other, and as a result there is something fundamentally unsatisfactory in the way these centrally placed characters are presented to the reader. There is a tendency for the focus to blur at crucial stages in the description of their moral development, and when this happens the picture we get of them looks uncannily like that glazed sympathetic smile emerging from the chalk marks of Sir Frederic's portrait.

The good negative thing that can be said of *Silas Marner* is that until Eppie grows up, three quarters of the way through it, none of these faults appears. There are no plaster saints, and there are no St. Theresas of Arbury Hall Farm on display. But there is plenty of evidence of more positive aspects of George Eliot's personality and genius, which, on the basis of a reading of the other novels, one might have thought were inextricably bound up with these faults. There is a sympathetic understanding of human weakness that too often seems inseparable from certain habits of condescension and moral uplift in her earlier novels. There is a calm contemplation of the inevitable consequences of moral slackness and thoughtless self-indulgence, but without the smug "I told you so's" tagged on at the end of them. And there is a scrupulous attention to the minutiae of motive, the subtle shifts of deception and self-deception, which complicate our responses to her characters' lives. In addition there is her unspectacular and utterly convincing representation of ordinary life bumping along from day to day and from season to season, in the provincial circumstances of her cast of English Midland village characters. No one has done this better than George Eliot does it here.

This is not to say that George Eliot does not reveal herself as a moralist in *Silas Marner*. She does make moral judgments, which do issue from analyses of the minds and motives of her characters. But she does not confuse the morally charged and the morally neutral aspects of her story. This combination of moral passion and curiosity about both the interior and exterior lives of her characters is what makes *Silas Marner* still worth reading, in such changed historical circumstances as today's.

3

Critical Reception

By the time she came to write *Silas Marner* in 1860, George Eliot was among the most celebrated novelists of her day. Only Dickens and Thackeray regularly sold more copies of their novels than she did, and they had begun writing in the 1830s, more than 20 years before George Eliot published her *Scenes of Clerical Life* (1858). Her reputation was made by her second work of fiction, *Adam Bede*, in 1859. This sold 16,000 copies in its first year of publication. John Blackwood, her publisher, was very pleased with the novel's reception. The success of its sales cemented the professional as well as personal relationship between publisher and author, which, with the exception of the publication of *Romola*, was to persist until Blackwood's death. *Silas Marner* was published by Blackwood after the slightly disappointing returns on her second novel, *The Mill on the Floss* (1860), and it was an immediate critical success. Publication in the mid-nineteenth century was often preceded by subscription, and in this case Blackwood achieved a total subscription of 5,000 copies, which was a large figure (for *Adam Bede* he had managed only 730). This is partly to be explained by the popularity of her earlier work and partly by the fact that the story sold in a single volume edition at 12 shillings per copy.

Critical Reception

By 1861, 8,000 copies had been sold. George Eliot received £1,760 in royalties, which had been fixed at 33 percent. It was a great deal of money for an author to receive in the 1860s and confirmed the preeminent place she now occupied in the ranks of the first-generation novelists of the 1850s and 1860s.

By this time reviewers knew that "George Eliot" was none other than Marian Evans, the atheistical contributor to the *Westminster Review* and translator of Strauss and Feuerbach. Her identity had come as a shock when it was discovered between readings of *Adam Bede* and *The Mill on the Floss*. This was because, contrary to expectation, it turned out to be both nonclerical and female. *Silas Marner*, therefore, was the first book George Eliot published after her identity was known and the immediate shock of that knowledge had worn off. Most reviewers were enormously relieved by what they found in it. This was the George Eliot they knew from *Scenes from Clerical Life* and *Adam Bede*, without the superaddition of those disagreeable features—e.g., the psychological inconsistency and sexual immorality hinted at in the character of the grown-up Maggie Tulliver—that had distressed readers of *The Mill on the Floss*.

It was the almost unanimous opinion of the reviewers that *Silas Marner* was "charming." The anonymous reviewer of the *Dublin University Magazine* was alone in his excoriation of George Eliot's treatment of rural life.[1] No one else was of the opinion that "it is not improving to live for ever in close contemplation of pigsties and refuseheaps" (Carroll, 192), which, in any case, are nowhere apparent in *Silas Marner*. On the contrary, several Victorian reviewers were very wise, as well as complimentary, about George Eliot's description of humble life. The author of the *Saturday Review* notice, for example, makes a much better contrast between George Eliot's and Sir Walter Scott's treatment of the poor than the *Dublin Magazine* makes between the dance and tea party scenes of *Silas Marner* and Oliver Wendell Holmes's *Elsie Venner*.[2] He is aware both of the special temptations (to condescension and invitation to moral improvement) offered by the subject of poverty in "quiet English parishes" and of the means by which George Eliot avoids them. And he is very shrewd about her observation of the frankness of the poor when he notes: "They say what they have to say, and do not mince matters. This is the rudeness of persons who do not mean to be rude; for they do not dream of the rules which a consideration for the feelings of others teaches those who are more refined" (Carroll, 170–76). This reviewer does share, though, the well-nigh universal misconception that the villagers of Raveloe *are* poor (see the discussion in chapter 6). R. H. Hutton, in the *Economist* (April 1861), is one of the few exceptions to the rule here. He is also the only contemporary reviewer of *Silas Marner* to notice the way the conversation of the villagers in the Rainbow has a wider relation to the themes of the novel than is at first apparent. He anticipates Leslie Stephen's brilliant account of the parallels between the different strands of the conversation and topics of interest in contemporary intellectual and philosophical circles, in his *Cornhill* obituary article of February 1881.[3]

Stephen's article is one of three general essays published in the nineteenth-century reviews that still make interesting reading on George Eliot and have useful things in particular to say about *Silas Marner*. The others are by Richard Simpson in the *Home and Foreign Review* of October 1863, and by Henry James in the *Atlantic Monthly* of May 1885. Leslie Stephen articulated the fairly general opinion of George Eliot, which we have already found among earlier critics: that her work is at its best when it is at its most charming and that the charm tends to reside more in the early work than in the later. He is not stupid or sentimental about this. He knows more is required than charm alone, and he has interesting things to say about the different skills George Eliot displays in handling the "exposition" and "catastrophe" of her plots. He is perceptive also about her tendency to substitute elaborate analysis for direct presentation. These matters are illustrated with material from *Silas Marner*, referring especially to the relationship between the first and second parts of the novel (an issue introduced by E. S. Dallas in his review in the *Times* of April 1861). Even so, he thinks that it is the charm of scenes like the one in the Rainbow (chapter 6) that makes her novels utterly distinctive: "The sphere which she made specially her own is that quiet country life which she knew in early youth. Nobody has approached George Eliot in the power of seizing its essential characteristics and exhibiting its real charm" (Carroll, 464). Stephen makes a fair effort at explaining how this charm manages to coexist with more than a degree of intellectual rigor and ethical sensibility in *Silas Marner*, but the placing of the emphasis here does have the effect of simplifying the picture George Eliot provides of life in Raveloe. The same, I am afraid, is true of Henry James, who finds in *Silas Marner* a quality that "seems gilded by a sort of autumn haze, afternoon light, of meditation, which mitigates the sharpness of portraiture" (Carroll, 499). No doubt he would have elaborated on this metaphorical description of the charm of the novel if he had had occasion to write a review of it, but he never did, and so we have to glean what we can from passing references in his reviews of other, later, novels; and these turn out to be brief, inconclusive, and vaguely complimentary in the same idyllic terms.

The best Victorian criticism of *Silas Marner* is contained in the long essay by Richard Simpson in the *Home and Foreign Review*.[4] In the present writer's opinion this is the best thing ever written on George Eliot. In 30 pages Simpson methodically works his way though all of the novels up to and including *Romola* (the essay was written in the year of the novel's publication), examining with great subtlety the interrelated difficulties she tries to overcome in the three areas of plot, description and dialogue, and characters. What he says about *Silas Marner* is illuminating, but it is very difficult to detach his comments on this novel from what he says about George Eliot's other works. Simpson writes as a Roman Catholic and is therefore skeptical of George Eliot's attempts to separate both the outward forms of Christian (usually Protestant) belief and the inner core of Christian doctrine from the fundamental religious feeling that each of these things suggests but to which neither of them is essential. This he sees (rightly) as the basic principle underlying most of her and Lewes's theoretical work and all of her own novels. Simpson is acute in drawing attention to the scientific positivism that suffuses George Eliot's writing. He concedes that "it is no small victory to show that the godless humanitarianism of Strauss and Feuerbach can be made to appear the living centre of all the popular religions" (Carroll, 225), and his admiration for the extent to which George Eliot's literary skill makes up the deficit of her intellectual error, as he perceives it, is genuine. *Silas Marner*, for example, "moved among peasants and rustic squires, doctors, farmers, and parsons. Its moral and even religious tendency appeared unexceptionable; and the interest of the story was concentrated in a wonderful way in the psychological change of the weaver from superstition, through infidelity, to faith" (Carroll, 226). The "interest of the story" is then explained in a single paragraph I will quote in full in order to give some idea of the flair and brilliance of Simpson's argument:

> The secondary plot, which remains in quite elemental and zoophytic form in the *Mill on the Floss*, becomes more highly organised in *Silas Marner*. It is necessary, for the development of the weaver's character, that he should become a miser, lose his gold, recover somewhat of his neighbours' good-will by misfortune, find a child, and be restored to social life by love. It was congruous, too, that he should find his gold again at last. Now to make all these accidents happen just in the nick of time only because they were wanted, would be feeble in the extreme; but if a secondary plot is introduced, out of which they naturally grow, they lose their arbitrary character, and are felt to be in place. Hence the secondary hero, Godfrey Cass, is introduced, as the centre of a plot which naturally bears fruit in the theft of Marner's gold, in throwing the child on his hands, and in restoring his hoard when it has been supplanted by a living idol as the object of his devotion. George Eliot surrounds herself with a mystic Egyptian darkness, and we approach her temple through an avenue of sphinxes; but it is not impossible to discover the irony of making Marner's conversion depend altogether on human sympathies and love, while he, simple fellow, fails to see the action of the general law of humanity, and attributes every thing to the "dealings" which regulate the accidents. *Silas Marner* contains an apology for Providence arbitrary and petitionary as the silliest of religious novels, and an apology for the special doctrines of Feuerbach's humanitarianism worked up with the utmost dialectic and psychological ability. There is great ingenuity in this method of planting opinions which one wishes to eradicate, and of hiding a subtle argument for error under a specious defence of the truth. (Carroll, 229)

Simpson is equally incisive about character and, especially, the varying quality of the description and dialogue in *Silas Marner*. He draws fine distinctions between wit and humor, epigrams and proverbs, arguing that George Eliot "makes excellent proverbs, and poor epigrams" (Carroll, 233). He discovers the origins of her characters' proverbial speech in Dickens and Shakespeare, and in precise references to literary sources like the records of a contemporary law case (the Swinfen will) and the performance of a contemporary play (Tom Taylor's *Our American Cousin*)—both of these sources providing material for the villagers' conversation in the Rainbow. To a non-Catholic, the foundations of Simpson's argument against George Eliot feel as firm today as they must have felt to his Catholic readers more than a century ago. And the superstructure of commentary on the detail of her novels, *Silas Marner* included, is equally impressive. Add to these things the brio and exuberance of his style, and you have one of the most remarkable critical documents of the Victorian age. David Carroll offers the whole of it in his *Critical Heritage* volume on George Eliot. A reading will tell you as much about *Silas Marner* as any shelfful of more recent books on the subject.

In fact after the Victorians, indeed after George Eliot's death in 1881, there is little outside Henry James worth reading on George Eliot until Virginia Woolf wrote her famous essay in the *Times Literary Supplement* in 1919, and this said nothing about *Silas Marner*. Virginia Woolf sought to recommend George Eliot as the person who had written Middlemarch, "one of the few English novels written for grown up people,"[5] and during the next 30 years this became the accepted wisdom. The fact that it also happened to be true shouldn't be allowed to disguise the comparative neglect of the earlier work up to and including *Silas Marner*.

This neglect is observable in full-length books like those of Gerald Bullett (*George Eliot: Her Life and Books*) and Joan Bennett (*George Eliot: Her Mind and Her Art*), as it is also in what is probably the most searching work of modern criticism on George Eliot, F. R. Leavis's essay in *The Great Tradition*.[6] There are only two pages on *Silas Marner* here. It is described as a "minor masterpiece" that "has in it, in its solid way, something of the fairy-tale" (Leavis 1948, 46). Really, the appreciation is not much of an advance on Leslie Stephen, in spite of the carping tone in which Stephen's views on the novel are deplored:

"The mood of enchanted adult reminiscence blends with the re-captured traditional aura to give the world of *Silas Marner* its atmosphere" (Leavis 1948, 46). That was Stephen's view, too. But now, by implication, these phrases are placed in a questionable light. Leavis's remarks on *Silas Marner* are there to prepare the way for more admiring judgments on the later novels. *Silas Marner*, then, is damned with faint praise in comparison with these.

Queenie Leavis, though, seems to have entertained a higher opinion of this novel than her husband did. Her Penguin Classics edition of the text, with excellent notes and a searching introductory essay, makes a great deal more of the "fairy-tale" element than he does and manages to place *Silas Marner* more centrally in the tradition of writing about the "organic community" than he seems to have thought was appropriate.[7] Her point is made through comparisons between the picture of peasant life in Raveloe and the description of the same thing in a chapter on "The Peasant System" in George Sturt's *Change in the Village*.[8] This is a book about English rural life in the nineteenth century as seen from the vantage point of a man who has run a wheelwright's business in the small town of Farnham in Surrey (southern England). There is some controversy about the extent to which Sturt's picture of village life, "the home-made civilization of the rural English," is an accurate reflection of its subject. John Holloway, for example, in his equally thoughtful introduction to the Everyman edition of the novel (1975),[9] suggests that "George Eliot's picture of Raveloe is somewhat idealized" (Holloway, vii), and this would suggest that Sturt's south-country picture is idealized too. Queenie Leavis, though, insists on the correctness as well as the inherent value of the habits of "neighbourliness" and rustic charity that are demonstrated by the Maceys, the Winthrops, and the rest of the Raveloe community. Silas's restoration at the end of Part 1 is qualified by the fact that he "never does acquire the pieties inborn with the villagers. He gets along eventually by adopting all the village customs without questioning them, but never, of course, has the traditional associations which make people benefit by them" (Leavis 1967, 24). This is a view of the matter that needs to be carefully tested against the representation of village life in Raveloe throughout *Silas Marner*, as well as against what we can discover about rural society in the Midland counties of England during the decades immediately before and after the turn of the eighteenth century, outside the pages of Sturt and a few others. (A good place to start is Flora Thompson's *Lark Rise* books (1939–1963) about village life on the Oxfordshire-Northamptonshire border at the turn of the nineteenth century. There are interesting comments, too, in chapters 16, 17, and 21 of Raymond Williams's *The Country and the City* [1973].) It is almost certainly the case that Queenie Leavis's observations about the organic community in Raveloe are as idealized as George Eliot's description of that community, and this does produce a rather unbalanced reading of the novel. Given its terms of reference, though, Queenie Leavis's essay is an excellent piece of writing, crammed full of detailed information about the working and domestic lives of the fictional population.

The details Queenie Leavis ignores are amply compensated for in John Holloway's introduction to the Everyman edition. Holloway is very informative about the condition of linen weavers in the late eighteenth to mid-nineteenth centuries. He has examined the *Final Report* of the *Royal Commission on the Condition of the Handloom Weavers* (1841), Thom's *Rhymes and Recollections of a Handloom Weaver* (1845), and books like Peter Gaskell's *Artisans and Machinery* (1836), and A. J. Warden's *The Linen Trade* (1864). His conclusion is that George Eliot's picture of the changing fortunes of linen weavers from the 1790s to the 1830s is both accurate and well adapted to the narrative of Silas's move to Raveloe, his success in establishing himself there as a hand-loom weaver, and his good luck in retrieving his money at a time when his services as a weaver would have been less in demand as a result of increasing competition from factory power-loom weavers from the 1820s onward. (The details are given on pages x–xiii of this edition.) To my mind Holloway's identification of Lantern Yard with the congregational churches of North Warwickshire is less convincing, as will be evident from my treatment of this aspect of the novel in chapter 5. He is interesting, though, on George Eliot's use of metaphors from contemporary studies in geology, and its link with "the widespread mid-Victorian sense of long-term and inconspicuous, but profound causal process as the key to experience" (Holloway, xvii).

The Leavis and Holloway editions of *Silas Marner* contain the best of modern criticism of the novel. R. P. Draper's "Casebook" on *Silas Marner* and *The Mill on the Floss* (1977) shows how mediocre (and difficult to find) most of the rest has been. An exception must be made, though, of David Carroll, whose essay on the debt to Feuerbach, "Revising the Oracles of Religion" offers useful insights into the relationship between the Cass and Marner stories and into the positivist background to George Eliot's arrangement of the plot. Simpson had made the point a hundred years earlier, and Carroll is generous in his acknowledgment of this.[10] Still, it is a sobering thought about the progress of criticism that the best we can do to appreciate this novel, apart from reading it with pleasure, is to consult the moldering pages of a nineteenth-century Catholic periodical that folded after two year's publication for want of a wide enough contemporary readership.

A READING

4

Preface: The Epigraph

Silas Marner was first published in 1861 with a title page that included an epigraph of three lines from Wordsworth:

> A child, more than all other gifts
> That earth can offer to declining man,
> Brings hope with it, and forward-looking thoughts.[1]

The reference is clearly to Silas's attachment to Eppie. It is her arrival at his door that gives him the hope and forward-looking thoughts that banish his misery at the theft of his guineas. The lines are taken from "Michael," a brief narrative poem that first appeared in the second edition of *The Lyrical Ballads* in 1800. Michael's experience is the reverse of Silas's. He is an old shepherd living with his wife and son in a cottage on the slopes of Grasmere Vale. Like Silas he experiences a financial misfortune, but unlike Silas he allows it to separate him from the child he loves most dearly. In an attempt to mend the family fortunes Luke, the boy, goes off to the city and comes to no good. This is a shattering blow to the old man, who spends the last years of his life in a state of dazed incomprehension at what has happened to him. Both stories are about the close emotional bond between fathers and children. But in George Eliot's novel there are two fathers. Silas is the father whose "decline" is arrested by the arrival of what becomes his own child. Godfrey Cass, on the other hand, is the father who refuses the gift of his child, the offspring of his union with Molly Farren. His decline begins with the discovery of this child and the punishment that comes in the form of his sterile marriage to Nancy Lammeter. What he and Nancy both lack in the second part of *Silas Marner* is precisely that "hope ... and forward-looking thoughts" that the much older Silas possesses as a result of his taking upon himself the role of father to Godfrey's child.

Wordsworth's poetry had been George Eliot's favorite reading from an early age. The themes that gripped her imagination were those Wordsworth had expressed in verse more than half a century before she wrote any of her novels. The stories of *The Lyrical Ballads* are all about those close family ties and responsibilities that she had made the subject of her own stories as early as *Adam Bede* and that are at the center of both of the main plots of *Silas Marner*. Molly Farren's situation, for example, is a compound of that of Wordsworth's Mad Mother and of Martha Ray in "The Thorn":

> And they had fix'd the wedding-day
> That morning that must wed them both;
> But Stephen to another maid
> Had sworn another oath.[2]

The familiar story from the ballads Wordsworth is imitating links Martha's experience here with Molly's in George Eliot's novel. True, Molly weds Godfrey (an unlikely thing to happen, but Regency poetry readers could stomach what Victorian novel readers would have turned in horror from their doors), and she doesn't hang her child. Her situation is more like that of the anonymous Mad Mother:

> Dread not their taunts, my little life!
> I am thy father's wedded wife;

> And underneath the spreading tree
> We two will live in honesty.
> If his sweet boy he could forsake,
> With me he never would have stay'd:
> From him no harm my babe can take,
> But he, poor man! is wretched made.[3]

Parents' feelings for their children are reciprocated by children's feelings for their parents both in Wordsworth and in George Eliot. Eppie's wish for a humble working life with Aaron and her father, in preference to an altogether more elevated position with Godfrey and Nancy at the Red House, is anticipated by little Edward's preference for his "quaint house" at Kilve shore over the woods and green hills of "sweet Liswyn shore" in Wordsworth's "Anecdote for Fathers." Edward's little white lie about the weather cock (he pretends that he doesn't like the weather cock at Liswyn) is intended to hide his deep attachment to his own home and family. It is this sort of instinctive feeling for family pieties and local affiliations that makes children like Edward the "best philosophers" of Wordsworth's later "Immortality Ode." The father's appreciation of his son's native wisdom is not unlike Silas's feeling for Eppie and the lesson in love he has learned from her presence in his cottage:

> Oh dearest, dearest boy! my heart
> For better love would seldom yearn
> Could I but teach the hundredth part
> Of what from thee I learn.[4]

In *Silas Marner* attachment to the child prepares the way for wider attachments to the village community at Raveloe. In its turn it has been prepared for by attachment to objects. The possibility of Silas's feeling for Eppie is foreshadowed in his feeling for the brown earthenware pot that had been his companion for 12 years before it is broken, shortly before the theft of the gold. It is said to be "his most precious utensil" (69) and is described in terms very like those with which Wordsworth had described the lamps Michael's father used to light up the cottage during evenings spent with his family in "eager industry." Like the pot, the lamp is spoken of "minutely." It is an "aged utensil which had perform'd / Service beyond all others of its kind" ("Michael," 117–18). A little later it is described as the "Surviving Comrade of uncounted hours," just as Silas's pot was the "companion" of his own. After he has broken his pot, Silas sticks the bits together and "propped the ruin in its old place for a memorial" (69). Wordsworth's poems are full of things that stand as memorials to the unforgotten intimacies of the past. In "Michael," the sheepfold that the shepherd and his son were building before Luke's trip to London stands as just such a memorial to their companionship. The poem ends with the cottage in ruins, but "the remains / Of the unfinished Sheepfold may be seen / Beside the boisterous brook of Green-head Gill" ("Michael," 489–91). Almost at the end of *Silas Marner* Silas and Eppie return from Raveloe to Lantern Yard to seek out the chapel from which Silas had been expelled all those years ago. There is no sign of it. A factory has been built on the site. This seems to be a suitable end to a sorry experience of misguided religious enthusiasm in Silas's youth. But even here a single building—"the house with the o'erhanging window" (240)—is just the same, attesting to the memory's need to find some Wordsworthian anchor even in the unpropitious circumstances of alienation and despair.

Wordsworth insists that devoting so many lines to the description of Michael's lamp is not a "waste of words." George Eliot, too, prefaces her description of the pot with an indication of its near-allegorical significance. The breaking of it is "a little incident . . . which showed that the sap of affection was not all gone" (69). There follows a clear, unfussy account of the position of the pot, its use, and the bold outline of its shape, which eases us very gently into an understanding of its importance to Silas. It always stood on the same spot, we are told, "always lending its handle to him in the early morning" (69). The word "lending" there comes very naturally. We can take it simply as a statement about the position of the handle, sticking out toward Silas because that is how he would have left it, ready for use next day. But the word can be made to suggest that the pot is actually doing something. The participial form half animates it. So when we are told later in the same sentence that "its form had an expression for him of willing helpfulness, and the impress of its handle on his palm gave satisfaction," we register the fancy that Silas and the pot fit together in a way that is more like a human relationship than a mere connection between a human being and an object.

This, too, is part of George Eliot's inheritance from Wordsworth. Unfortunately the only pot that comes to mind from the poet is the pitcher carried on the head of the girl the poet sees forcing her way against the wind in the eleventh book of *The Prelude*, and there the particular circumstances don't favor a description of the relationship between the person and the object. But look at the Old Cumberland Beggar's staff, or the things in Margaret's house and garden in "The Ruined Cottage," and the link with George Eliot is clear. Both authors write best when they write most plainly. Margaret's wooden bowl, the beggar's staff, Silas's brown pot, and Nancy Lammeter's drab cloak and bonnet have the sturdy presence and the sense of having been used that George Eliot admired in the genre paintings and still lifes of the seventeenth century Dutch masters. Fortunately she didn't seek to emulate Wordsworth's practice of incorporating this in verse. She almost did. In a letter to her publisher about *Silas Marner* she wrote, "I have felt all through as if the story would have lent itself best to metrical rather than prose fiction."[5] We may be lucky, then, that *Silas Marner* didn't turn out to be one of those insipid narrative poems that contemporaries such as Tennyson produced in work like "Aylmer's Field" or "The Gardener's Daughter." George Eliot enjoyed writing verse, and she always did it badly. But the fact that she saw the subject of *Silas Marner* as a poetic one reinforces the view that much of what is best in it has less to do with the conventions of Victorian novel writing than with narrative conventions that came down to to her from quite another source, or sources.

5

Lantern Yard

In the same letter to her publisher in which she expressed her preference for a poetic treatment of her subject, George Eliot explained that the story "came to me first of all, quite suddenly, as a sort of legendary tale, suggested to me by my recollections of having once, in early childhood, seen a linen-weaver with a bag on his back."[1] Later this same publisher, John Chapman, wrote to his wife that " 'Silas Marner' sprang from her childish recollection of a man with a stoop and expression of face that led her to think that he was an alien from his fellows" (*Letters*, 427). It is not surprising, then, that just such a figure appears in the second sentence of the novel, "bent under a heavy bag" (51), which represents to the onlooker a "mysterious burden." Four pages later, in the same chapter, the figure is identified as Silas Marner, viewed by Jem Rodney, the mole catcher, "leaning against a stile with a heavy bag on his back" (55). He appears once more in the novel as a burdened traveler, at the beginning of chapter 5, where he is discovered a hundred yards away from his cottage as Dunstan Cass is escaping with the guineas. He is plodding along from the village "with a sack thrown round his shoulders as an overcoat" (90) against the evening chill. He had forgotten he needed a piece of fine twine in order to set up some new work in his loom in the morning and had gone out to buy it in Raveloe.

The first of these descriptions of the man with the bag is the most disturbing. The burden he carried is "mysterious" and his "alien-looking" aspect is emphasized. He belongs to a "region of vagueness and mystery." The shepherd who passes him on the road associates him with "the Evil One." This figure sounds most like the one George Eliot described in the letters. He sounds like a "legendary figure," and the fact that he was an "alien from his fellows" is mentioned in both the letter and the book. Of course at this early stage he is not identified with Silas. A little earlier still we were told that Silas was such a linen weaver. The anonymous figure's eccentric habits have been explained as the expression of his state of loneliness, and this has done something to disguise his legendary status and to assimilate him into the world of ordinary human beings. Even before this, George Eliot's childish recollection has been put in its place as the picture summoned to mind by the "brawny country folk" who are by no means identical to the little girl who is now the famous author writing her novel in the comfortable surroundings of her house in Blandford Square.

The second description, from the point of view of the mole catcher, is couched in less melodramatic terms. But it is made to sound strange because Silas is seen here having one of his cataleptic fits, and this too has the effect of removing him out of the ordinary run of things and making him into a peculiar figure of folk legend. Mr. Macey thinks that "there might be such a thing as a man's soul being loose from his body, and going out and in, like a bird out of its nest and back" (55), and who are the rest of the villagers to gainsay him? The next thing we are told is how Silas has cured Sally Oates's bad heart, a misguided act that has added to his already considerable reputation for eccentricity. By the time we come to the third description, Silas's catalepsy has been given a medically respectable explanation. The bag on his back—which was mysterious on its first appearance, and peculiar on its second one only by virtue of the fact that in the middle of his fit Silas had not thought to rest it against the stile he was leaning on—is just a piece of old sacking that is performing an obviously useful function in keeping out the cold. The anonymous figure of legend has been converted into the linen weaver called Silas Marner and, in the process, has been transformed from the countrymen's devil's apprentice into our own historically and biographically explained village craftsman. In doing this, however, George Eliot has not altogether let go of his legendary properties. The picture that was stamped on her mind at the outset stays there to the end, even though its bold and simple outline is for much of the time filled in with subtler shades and softened with more muted colors.

Apart from her memories of traveling linen weavers in the Warwickshire lanes of her childhood, there is one other place where George Eliot would have encountered a strange man with a bag on his back. That is in the first page of *The Pilgrim's Progress*, Bunyan's story of Christian's journey from the City of Destruction to the Celestial City.[2] There Bunyan's dreamer beholds "a man clothed with rags, standing in a certain place, with his face from his own house, a book in his hand, and a great burden upon his back" (Bunyan, 39). This man, the pilgrim, deliberately flees from his own land to seek salvation elsewhere. The burden on his back is his conviction of sin, which falls from him when he discovers the Cross: "So I saw in my dream, that just as Christian came up with the Cross, his burden loosed from off his shoulders, and fell from off his back" (Bunyan, 69–70). Silas also turns his back on his own country and finds a sort of salvation elsewhere, at Raveloe. His burden is not so much conviction of sin as a sense of righteousness impeached by the sins of others. But it has the same effect of cutting him off from other men. He fails, however, to discover on his journey such fellow seekers after righteousness as Faithful and Hopeful. Even in Raveloe he is to spend 15 years of his life isolated with his disbelief in the good of either God or man. When Eppie comes to him, and the current of feeling begins to flow again in his heart, the situation is described in the same language of seventeenth-century allegory as Bunyan used in his account of the end of Christian's journey: "In old days there were angels who came and took men by the hand and led them away from the City of Destruction. We see no white-winged angels now. But yet men are led away from threatening destruction: a hand is put into theirs, which leads them forth gently toward the calm and bright land, so that they look no more backward; and the hand may be a little child's" (190–91). The white-winged angels are the two Shining Ones at the gate of the Heavenly City in Bunyan's parable. They led Christian up "by the arms" from the River that surrounded the City," and the City "shone like the sun" as he entered it (Bunyan, 204).

By imitating Bunyan's language so closely, George Eliot is insisting on the character of her story as a secular fable demythologizing his puritan allegory. This doesn't merely involve the substitution of bags of linen for burdens of sin, and an orphan child for the shining angels. It also involves a quite different way of looking at and accounting for those impulses of the human mind to which we still attach words like "sin," "guilt," "right," "crime," and, by George Eliot's time, "loneliness" and "alienation." The daughter of a low-church Anglican land agent in the Victorian West Midlands looks at these things in a very different light from a nonconformist tinker in the East Midland countryside of the late seventeenth century. But she shares enough of an inheritance with him to ground her story in the same form of a parable of expulsion, travel, and resettlement as Bunyan used for his account of the experience of the true Christian in *The Pilgrim's Progress*.

She does this in spite of the fact that her character's experience is at first one of mistrust and ill-use at the hands of what appears to be just such a religious community as Bunyan belonged to and ministered to in Bedford. We are never told what precise denomination the Lantern Yard community belongs to. It is described in chapter 2 as "a narrow religious sect," a "little hidden world" that calls itself a "church" (56). "Narrow" and "hidden" immediately betray George Eliot's critical judgment. But she implies in the same paragraph that in secular terms the community has much to recommend it, because in it "the poorest layman has the chance of distinguishing himself by gifts of speech, and has, at the very least, the weight of a silent voter in the government of his community." It is not just the prevailing sentiments of a contemporary political culture that will see some virtue in an institution working in accordance with this democratic spirit. George Eliot the liberal radical sees it too. It later becomes clear, however, that the habit of silent voting can take a pernicious form. The religious superstition that the institution exists to safeguard tends to undermine all that is most progressive and forward-looking in its political arrangements. This is to be Silas's experience before he escapes to Raveloe. Therefore, to understand the state of mind in which Silas is found before the theft of his guineas, we need to discover more about his life in Lantern Yard by looking more closely at the community George Eliot describes in the first chapter of the novel.

In order to do that, we must read back into it what we find out about Silas's early religious experiences from his conversations with Dolly Winthrop much later on, after his guineas have been stolen, in chapter 10 and after he has adopted Eppie, in chapter 14. In chapter 10 Silas reads out the letters I. H. S. on the lardy cakes Dolly has baked for him, and this is taken as evidence of his learning, that is, that he can read. But we are told that he was "as unable to interpret the letters as Dolly" (136); so, unsurprisingly, this aspect of a more ritualistic religion than his own (the letters are a monogram representing a contraction of the Greek spelling of "Jesus") makes no impression on him. George Eliot's intention might have been an ironic one here, though, because these first three letter of the name of the redeemer were often interpreted as the initials of "Jesus Hominum Salvator" or "In Hac (cruce) Salvus" (Latin for "Jesus Savior of Men" and "In This (Cross) Salvation"). In other words they emphasized the message of Christ that Lantern Yard believed was all-important: the "Assurance of salvation" that had earlier been the topic of Silas's conversations with William Dane.

Silas explains to Dolly that although there were many churches in the town he came from, he did not attend them, but a "chapel," in which Christmas was celebrated no more specially than any other day of the year. Thus, in chapter 14, when Dolly tries to persuade him to have Eppie christened, Silas is puzzled by the word because "he had only heard of baptism, and had only seen the baptism of grown men and women." (182). The "Bible name" he wants to give the baby is

Hephzibah, an Old Testament name from the Book of Isaiah (62:4), which means "my delight in her," and is the prophet's new name for Jerusalem: "Thou shalt no more be termed Forsaken; neither shall thy land any more be termed Desolate: but thou shalt be called Hephzibah, and thy land Beulah: for the Lord delighted in thee." The application to Eppie (Silas's shortened form of the name) is clear. Less clear is why his mother and deceased sister should also have borne the name, except that its provenance in Isaiah links Silas's upbringing with the book in the Old Testament most often read by the Puritans as foreshadowing the coming of Christ in the New Testament, and which therefore contains a great deal of matter conforming to their own views on the salvation of his chosen people: "And I will bring forth a seed out of Jacob, and out of Judah an inheritor of my mountains: and mine elect shall inherit it, and my servants shall dwell there" (Isaiah 65:9). Even in naming the source of his personal, secular salvation, Silas comes close to attributing to it the harsher doctrines of his earlier religious training.

The distinction between baptism and christening also points in the direction of the narrow sectarian Puritanism of Bunyan's seventeenth century. Bunyan was a member of the Strict or Particular Baptists, who believed that Christ died only for the elect and that therefore there was no possibility of general atonement, only particular atonement for those predestined to be saved. Two consequences of this belief marked off the Particular Baptists from most of the other Reformed congregations. The first, which they shared with the General Baptists, who believed in a general atonement, was the baptism by immersion that Silas seems to be referring to in his conversation with Dolly Winthrop. The idea of adult baptism by immersion originated in John's baptism of Jesus recorded in three of the four gospels, where baptism is associated with repentance for the remission of sins. (See especially Mark 1:4 and Luke 3:3. Jesus appears to be giving an order of baptism at Matthew 28:19–20.) Most of the Christian churches, however, interpreted this to mean infant baptism, often simply by the pouring of water or making the sign of the cross in water on the infant's head. All Baptists, however, insisted on full immersion of the adult, who must be responsible enough to make a profession of faith before receiving baptism.

Although some other nonconformist groups also practised adult baptism, it seems likely that in 1790 or thereabouts the sect to which Silas belonged was Baptist. The reason for supposing that it was a Particular and not a General Baptist sect is partly the unforgiving character of the religion he has grown up in, as this is filtered through to us in what we hear about Silas's experiences, and partly the sense we have that it is nonevangelical. We hear nothing of the attempts of Lantern Yard to proselytize. Indeed its members seem to keep ostentatiously to themselves, marrying among themselves and even conducting a trial of one of their number who is suspected of theft. By the 1790s, the Particular Baptists had begun to be influenced by the Methodist revival with which George Eliot sympathized. They even founded a missionary society in 1792. Meanwhile their less fundamentalist fellow Baptists of the General persuasion had either undergone a sharp decline in membership or had merged with the new Unitarian church, which emphasized the humanity of Jesus in much the same way as George Eliot and the German theologians whose work she had translated had done. Her Coventry friends the Hennells were the free-thinking children of a Unitarian family. This makes Lantern Yard look like an even more exaggeratedly separatist and inward-turned congregation of true believers than we might have thought on first encountering it in *Silas Marner*.

Probably the most startling evidence of the character of Lantern Yard religion is the drawing of lots that persuades the community there that Silas is guilty of the theft of the church funds. The fact that the congregation took this measure (as well as prayer) to find out the truth, we are told, will surprise only "those who are unacquainted with that obscure religious life which has gone on in the alleys of our towns"(61). Silas thinks that by this means "his innocence [will be] certified by immediate divine interference (61)." There is not a great deal of evidence to show that any but the most extreme dissenting sects at the time these events in *Silas Marner* are supposed to be taking place (around 1790) would have searched for signs of God's favor or disfavor by the drawing of lots. The biblical justification of the practice must be the account of the battle between the armies of Saul and of the Philistines in 1 Samuel 14. There, Saul seeks to establish by the drawing of lots the identity of the man who disobeyed his order to refrain from eating food before the attack on the enemy. The culprit turns out to be his son Jonathan (see verses 40–42). He had not heard the order and had subsequently fed on honey from a honeycomb dropped by the departing Philistine army. Since there is a close parallel between Jonathan's and Silas's innocence of any deliberately immoral or illegal act, it is likely that George Eliot intended her readers, who were closer and more frequent readers of the Bible than we are, to pick up this reference. If they did, the comparison between Saul's and the Lantern Yard community's interpretation of the result of the lottery would again establish an ironic tone in the passage that works against the dissenters in much the same way as the letters on Dolly's lardy cakes are going to do several chapters further on.

In any event, the drawing of lots, far from appearing in the light of irreligious gambling (as it might to us), must have been a not untypical way for a fundamentalist sectarian chapel to behave. Along with the practice of extemporaneous prayer, it is the principal reason Holloway gives for supposing that Lantern Yard is Congregationalist: not that Congregationalists practiced the drawing of lots, but that they did believe "the decision of the congregation was the voice of Christ" (Holloway, xvi) and thus the drawing of lots would have been interpreted by them as the act of Christ working through the actions of his worshippers. But this would have been true of many nonconformist sects and all Calvinist ones. To the extent that she does place a great deal of emphasis on praying aloud without book and a severely democratic organization of church government, it may be that George Eliot has a Congregationalist assembly in mind and is associating it with the stricter forms of Calvinist worship that characterize most of the rest of what she tells us about the anonymous religion of Lantern Yard.

The search for signs of election, both in the inner soul and the outer circumstances of change and chance within which the soul makes its choices and decisions, is a familiar theme in the Puritan literature with which George Eliot was familiar. *The Pilgrim's Progress* is full of such searching. Most of Christian's entertainment at the "House of the Interpreter" takes the form, as its name suggests, of an inquiry into the significance of the pictures the Interpreter shows him. His conversation with the men and women he meets on the way often takes as its subject the true or false interpretations of signs of grace or damnation they have encountered during their own journeys. It is a short step from reacting to accidental signs of these things to artificially creating the circumstances in which interpretable signs will present themselves. That is what drawing of lots entails. It is all the more likely to happen where there is no priest, or intermediary between God and his congregation, to do the interpreting on the congregation's behalf. This is a part of the debit side of that democratic spirit George Eliot detected among her dissenters. It is a sign also of a rooted distrust on her part of the ability of ordinary people to arrive at sensible decisions without the guidance of some authority outside themselves. In *Silas Marner*, as we shall see, the source of authority is absent because the squire and the parson both fail to take responsibility for their charges. This has had a profound effect on the behavior of the village. Dolly Winthrop, it is true, behaves well to Silas after the theft of his guineas, and so do the other villagers, in their more grudging ways. But it took 15 years and a dramatic personal tragedy to alert them to Silas's need for companionship. There is more in common between their ignorance and the fanaticism of the Lantern Yard dissenters than at first appears.

The drawing of lots, the baptism by total immersion, the Old Testament names and practices, and the numerous ironies George Eliot establishes at the expense of such doctrines as election, salvation, and signs to be observed and interpreted all point to an identification of Lantern Yard with the most Calvinistic manifestations of late eighteenth-century English dissent. It is important to discriminate, here, between different strands in the English dissenting tradition George Eliot grew up with in her Warwickshire childhood. Queenie Leavis points us to J. S. Whale's *The Protestant Tradition* (1955), which tells us a lot about the theology and doctrines of Calvinism, but does not concern itself with English and specifically nonconformist traditions of worship. Since Queenie Leavis produced her edition of *Silas Marner*, Donald Davie has written an account of the history of dissent from the late seventeenth century to the present that is probably of greater interest to the literary student. He calls it *A Gathered Church*, and nobody will emerge from reading this book without a great deal of respect for varied manifestations of its subject.[3] Quite obviously the dissenting interest as a whole is not to be identified with the perverse and gloomy variant of it that is the community of Lantern Yard. Evidently this was not a mistake George Eliot could have made. Already, in the third of her *Scenes of Clerical Life*, she had produced a sympathetic study of an evangelical clergymen, Mr. Tryan, who, though not himself a dissenter, behaves in some ways not unlike one and is identified with the dissenting interest by most of his parishioners. And Dinah Morris, in George Eliot's first novel, *Adam Bede*, is a Methodist preacher painted in those glaringly ideal colors that speak more for George Eliot's goodness of heart than for her tact or intelligence. Her interest in both of these characters, though, shows how much she found to admire in types of nonconformity not entirely dissimilar to the one she represents in the descriptions of Lantern Yard.

The dissimilarity is more one of manner than of doctrine, though manner includes the degree of importance attributed to doctrine and the relationship between the kind of doctrine it is and the behavior deemed appropriate to individuals espousing it. What, then, was the Calvinist doctrine subscribed to by Lantern Yard? And what particular form does the evidence we have gleaned from George Eliot's description of it lead us to believe it takes in that community?

The core of Calvinist doctrine is the emphasis it places on a man's total responsibility for the conduct of his life. At the same time it stresses his total abjectness in the acknowledgment of the sin he shares with Adam, his first father, through the primal act of disobedience against God in the Garden of Eden. There is nothing positive that a man can do to earn remission of sin. The fact of election or nonelection precedes any act he can perform to deserve whatever status he enjoys, unbeknown to him. All he can do is *not* to behave in such a way as will reveal him as an unrepentant sinner, for the one thing that is certain is that without repentance no man can be saved, even if repentance is no guarantee that he will be saved.

In one of his dour religious tracts, Bunyan explains that "this Decree, Choice, or Election, was before the foundation of the World; and so before the Elect themselves had Being in themselves."[4] There is a more vivid illustration of the condition in Hopeful's words about faith and works near the end of *The Pilgrim's Progress*: "If a man runs a hundred pounds into a shop-keeper's debt, and after that shall pay for all that he shall fetch, yet his old debt stands still in the book uncrossed for the which the shop-keeper may sue him, and cast him into prison till he shall pay the debt" (Bunyan, 179). Each individual must search for evidence of election through the combined presence of repentance working in the soul and the grace of God revealing itself in signs in the world outside himself. To resume the image in Bunyan, he must look for the cross against his name in the shop-keeper's book, much as William Dane claims to have done in his conversation with Silas about "Assurance of salvation." Silas, the diffident and self-doubting tyro, confesses that "he could never arrive at anything higher than hope mingled with fear" (57), which one would assume to be the proper state of mind for a Puritan worshipper to have adopted. But William declares that "he had possessed unshaken assurance ever since, in the period of his conversion, he had dreamed that he saw the words 'calling and election sure' standing by themselves on a white page in the open Bible" (57–58). This sounds like another drawing of lots, with William practicing a kind of *sortes Virgilianae* on the scriptures (turning the pages of the Bible at random in hopes of finding comfort, guidance, and predictions of the future). William being the sort of hypocrite we later discover him to be, this is no doubt a parcel of lies as well as religious humbug. But in itself it was just the sort of searching for signs one associates with the more Calvinist-inclined of the puritan persuasion.

The fits that are the symptom of Silas's illness are bound to be interpreted by the congregation at Lantern Yard as signs of peculiar favor or disfavor with God. "Fit" is the word Mr. Macey uses to describe Silas's behavior, but when we are told how the fits first occurred at Lantern Yard they are described as "a mysterious rigidity and suspension of consciousness" (56). Later, when Eppie arrives at his cottage, he is "arrested . . . by the invisible world of catalepsy" (167), and it is as a cataleptic seizure or trance that his condition should be medically diagnosed. Even "catalepsy" is by now a rather archaic word used to describe a symptom of gross hysteria, and it is best to discuss it in a context of hysterical behavior familiar to George Eliot and to the neurologically well-informed Lewes.

Silas's condition sounds very like conversion hysteria (as it happens, a doubly suitable word to describe it in his case), so called because it converts mental distress into a physical illness characterized by paralysis of the limbs or other parts of the body. It also shares some of the characteristics of dissociative hysteria, where the sufferer experiences a loss of memory during a period of time that may well correspond with the hour or so that Silas stands rigid, having no idea afterward of what he has been doing. It was in treating the amnesia of his hysterical patient Anna O. that Joseph Breuer hit upon the practice of hypnotic suggestion that led to his and Freud's later interpretations of the subconscious mind, though it must be added that the amnesiac symptoms investigated by Freud and Breuer were not accompanied by the symptoms of physical paralysis apparent in the behavior of the conversion hysteric. Of course there is no suggestion here that in formulating Silas's history of religious enthusiasm, secular self-doubt, and symptoms of amnesiac hysteria (which she called "catalepsy") George Eliot anticipated Freud's theories of the unconscious. But there are more than accidental connections between those aspects of Silas's personality and his behavior, and it would be entirely consistent with the way his fortunes are portrayed in *Silas Marner* to read back into them the terminology of dissociative hysteria found in Freud's early studies of the condition.

What George Eliot was more likely to have had in the forefront of her mind, and what the congregation at Lantern Yard certainly must have had in the forefront of their minds, were the occasions in the gospels where Jesus is represented as healing the mentally ill. This is especially true of those suffering from the palsy, which is a sort of cerebral paralysis that has the effect of either removing the patient's control over his movements or prohibiting movement altogether. Silas undergoes an especially severe experience of this paralysis, so severe that Jem Rodney describes his eyes as being "set like a dead man's" (54). Mr. Macey says it is like "a man's soul being loose from his body, and going out and in, like a bird out of its nest and back" (55). This makes Silas's condition more like that of Jairus's daughter or the Lazarus of St. John, whom Jesus brought back from the dead. On the other hand, the experience of fits need not be a sign of peculiar grace. After all, Bunyan's Giant Despair sometimes had fits, though they were not accompanied by amnesia. Silas's amnesia, though, is there for the sake of the plot, to enable William Dane to cheat him over the money and for Eppie to be able to appear in the cottage without his having any idea how she got there. What Jem Rodney and the Lantern Yard people are impressed with is his immobility and deathlike appearance in his state of trance. Both Silas and the congregation consider this to be full of spiritual significance, and Silas to be "a brother selected for a peculiar discipline" (56). This might be a good or bad example to his fellow members of the chapel. Until the theft, they all believe that "its effect was seen in an accession of light and fervour" (56). They would have remembered Balaam in the Old Testament who "saw the vision of the Almighty, falling into a trance, but having his eyes open" (Numbers 24:4). Silas, though, knows that his outward trance is unaccompanied by any spiritual vision and doesn't pretend to what he has not in fact experienced. The status he enjoys in the community has no justification in any knowledge he acquires or witness he bears to suprarational truths of religion even as these are understood by Lantern Yard.

To establish the degree to which Silas's personality has been damaged by the narrow Calvinism in which he has been brought up, it is necessary to discriminate between different manifestations of late eighteenth-century dissent, which at first glance look very much the same. It makes a lot of difference, for example, whether views on election apply to particular members of a like-minded and self-protective sectarian group only or to mankind in general through the doctrine of general atonement. All dissent places heavy emphasis on election and salvation. But it is the distinctive feature of Lantern Yard dissent that it embraces the first of these with such fervor. A good example of emphasis on the second, within the Anglican church, is provided not in *Silas Marner*—where the rector, Mr. Crackenthorp, is a somewhat relaxed latitudinarian—but in Eliot's "Janet's Repentance," where Mr. Tryan, the new minister, is thought of as a dissenter and is judged by the townsfolk to be "the first Evangelical clergyman" to have risen above their horizon. He is associated with exhortation and prayer and is understood by his congregation to be a believer in "justification by faith alone,"[5] the acid test of Calvinist belief. One of the descriptions of his faith takes the form of a comparison between Arminianist (i.e., General Baptist) and Calvinist (i.e., Particular Baptist) views: "It is probable that . . . an Arminian with the toothache would prefer a skilful Calvinist dentist to a bungler staunch against the doctrines of Election and Final Perseverance."[6] Nevertheless, George Eliot's portrait of Tryan is a deeply sympathetic one, and this is because of the way his evangelical piety carries him beyond considerations of self to an outward-directed compassion for the sufferings of others.

This is precisely what is lacking in Lantern Yard, in spite of a similarity in doctrine. The culture Silas has shared with his congregation, we are told, "had not defined any channels for his sense of mystery, and so it spread itself over the proper pathway of inquiry and knowledge" (57). The "self-complacent suppression of inward triumph" that "lurked" in William Dane's eye and lips contrasts with "the expression of trusting simplicity" (57) in Silas's face. Silas has merged his own personality so completely with that of his coreligionists that he has no inner source of strength and support when they reject him. Since he knows that rejection is based on a lie, and the lie has been confirmed by a lottery that is, in his view, a valid expression of the beliefs he has shared with his community, there is no way in which he can reconcile the beliefs he has espoused with the innocence he knows he possesses. The selfishness of the group becomes apparent to one of its members only when he is forced into uncomfortable separation from it. Hence the "shaken trust in God and man" brought about by the result of the lottery creates in Silas a despair that is "little short of madness" (61). It is a despair that could not have been brought into existence by the evangelical religion represented by Mr. Tryan in "Janet's Repentance," however compromised that religion might be by narrow doctrines and moral hypocrisy.

The contrast can be made plain by looking at George Eliot's account of Milby evangelicalism in chapter 10 of "Janet's Repentance." The author has explained that "Evangelicalism was making its way into Milby, and gradually diffusing its subtle odour into chambers that were bolted and barred against it." Like other religious revivals, she says, it had a mixed effect, and it may be that "some of Mr. Tryan's hearers had gained a religious vocabulary rather than religious experience" (*Scenes*, 255). But that is by no means the whole story. The danger of hypocrisy is countered by the invitation to pass beyond the merely personal and selfish concerns of the separate individual. Indeed there can be no hypocrisy without at least the impetus to rise above oneself in this way, so hypocrisy has to be accepted as an unavoidable temptation to the man or woman who recognizes the call of duty. William Dane is not so much a hypocrite as a liar and a cheat. He does not deceive himself into supposing he really is as pious as he pretends to be. This is very different from the difficulties experienced by the Evangelicals of Milby in reconciling their natural selfishness with the duty of selfless concern for both the spiritual and material good of others:

> Evangelicalism had brought into palpable existence and operation in Milby society that idea of duty, that recognition of something to be lived for beyond the mere satisfaction of self, which is to the moral life what the addition of a great central ganglion is to animal life. No man can begin to mould himself on a faith or an idea without rising to a higher order of experience: a principle of subordination, of self-mastery, has been introduced into his nature; he is no longer a mere bundle of impressions, desires, and impulses. Whatever might be the weaknesses of the ladies who pruned the luxuriance of their lace and ribbons, cut out garments for the poor, distributed tracts, quoted Scripture, and defined the true Gospel, they had learned this—that there was a divine work to be done in life, a rule of goodness higher than the opinion of their neighbours; and if the notion of a heaven in reserve for themselves was a little

too prominent, yet the theory of fitness for that heaven consisted in purity of heart, in Christ-like compassion in the subduing of selfish desires. They might give the name of piety to much that was only puritan egoism; they might call many things sin that were not sin; but they had at least the feeling that sin was to be avoided and resisted, and colour-blindness, which may mistake drab for scarlet, is better than total blindness which sees no distinction of colour at all. (*Scenes*, 255–56)

Mr. Tryan's difficulties have a different origin from those of the worshippers at Lantern Yard. In seeking to detect it, though, George Eliot has recourse to a vocabulary similar to the one she will use to explain the damming up of Silas's own current of sympathy, both before and after the disappearance of the money:

The real heroes, of God's making, are quite different: they have their natural heritage of love and conscience which they drew in with their mother's milk; they know one or two of those deep spiritual truths which are only to be won by long wrestling with their own sins and their own sorrows; they have earned faith and strength so far as they have done genuine work: but the rest is dry barren theory, blank prejudice, vague hearsay. Their insight is blended with mere opinion; their sympathy is perhaps confined in narrow conduits of doctrine, instead of flowing forth with the freedom of a stream that blesses every weed in its course; obstinacy or self-assertion will often interfuse itself with their grandest impulses; and their very deeds of self-sacrifice are sometimes only the rebound of a passionate egoism. So it was with Mr. Tryan: and any one looking at him with the bird's-eye glance of a critic might perhaps say that he made the mistake of identifying Christianity with a too narrow doctrinal system; that he saw God's work too exclusively in antagonism to the world, the flesh, and the devil; that his intellectual culture was too limited—and so on; making Mr. Tryan the text for a wise discourse on the characteristics of the Evangelical school in his day. (*Scenes*, 256–57)

Silas experiences self-doubt in his Lantern Yard days, but he makes none of the effort to master it that we are shown in Milby society or in Mr. Tryan's wrestling with his own sins and sorrows. Silas's belief is as "benumbing" as his unbelief is later, when he recoils from what he had thought was the "divine judgement" of the lottery. Without being able to make "an effort of independent thought," he is not much more than a "mere bundle of impressions, desires, and impulses" the author of "Janet's Repentance" claims human beings must be in the absence of that extrapersonal principle directing them to the service of others. By shunning society and reducing himself to the status of a component in his working machinery—"getting into his loom"—he confirms the psychological authority still exercised by the religion in which he no longer believes. The sense of election is slow to disappear. It clings to the believer as a protection against an alien world long after he has ceased to acknowledge the reality of the religion of which it is the moral foundation. For, in psychological terms, what can election mean other than the practices of self-approval, self-justification and self-concern? George Eliot was fond of applying Feuerbach's theory of the religion of humanity to the conduct of her characters. This means that she interpreted the behavior of those characters in terms of the ways they apprehended the divinity outside them. Since Silas has allowed his knowledge of this divinity to be constrained by the narrow theories of Lantern Yard rather than foster his native piety, he has grown accustomed to worshiping a God simultaneously infinitely removed from him and judiciously interested in him alone. The picture of him that remains, then, when the God has been rejected, is correspondingly impoverished. He is an exile not only in terms of geography, but in terms of his own inner landscape. He is as estranged from all that is best in himself as he is from all that is worst in the religious community that, to all effects and purposes, expelled him.

6

Raveloe

Events in *Silas Marner* are represented in greater historical than geographical detail. The novel opens with a description of the time the story is supposed to be taking place, "In the days when the spinning-wheels hummed busily in the farmhouses . . ."; and the second paragraph opens with a reference to "the early years of this century." Silas arrived in Raveloe 15 years before the events recorded in it take place. This means that the flight from Lantern Yard must have occurred about 1790. All the information we are given about linen weaving as a cottage industry, the use of the winnowing machine for flax (invented in 1755), and Silas's weekly income growing to 250 guineas over 15 years is accurate, as is the suggestion that the weavers' prosperity was deteriorating in the 1820s, when the events of Part 2 are taking place. The "glorious war time" of chapter 3 accounts in large part for the general sense of material well-being we take away from Raveloe. The war referred to is the war against the French fought between 1793 and 1815, which places most of the events of *Silas Marner* in the years between the turn of the eighteenth century into the nineteenth century and the passing of the Reform Bill of 1832. This is George Eliot's favorite period setting for her novels. Only the last, *Daniel Deronda,* is set in the present. The choice of this period can be explained in two ways. It can be argued that George Eliot was interested in those years because they were years of social unrest and agitation resolved by the extension of the suffrage produced by the 1832 Act. This made an instructive parallel with the late 1850s and early 1860s, in which different forms of social agitation looked as if they were leading to a similar resolution, which did in fact occur in the form of the 1867 Reform Bill. Or it can be argued that George Eliot saw these years as years of quiet, with the country insulated against the wider conflict in Europe by the power of the British navy and protected from internal social pressures by the acquiescence of the rural population (of which she knew most) in the high price of homegrown corn.

The little we see of the urban background of Lantern Yard doesn't allow us to make a judgment about the extent of prosperity or poverty in the manufacturing towns. All we find out is that many factories have been built between the 1780s, when Silas was living there, and the 1820s, when he returns with Eppie. But there is no doubt at all that the countryside is flourishing. The countryfolk appear "brawny" by the side of the "pallid undersized men" (51) who have traveled from the towns. Raveloe was not, we are told, "one of those barren parishes lying on the outskirts of civilization." It was a rich, "important looking" village "nestled in a sunny well-wooded hollow" (53), its buildings described by epithets like "fine," "well-walled," and "imposing." An ironic note is struck not only by the proximity of "war time" and "liv[ing] in a rollicking fashion," "keeping a jolly good Christmas," etcetera, but also by the observation that all this was accomplished by farming badly and relying on the curbs on imports of foreign corn to maintain the high price of the villagers' own unsatisfactory product. The reader has to decide whether this is just a vague gesture in the direction of social and historical realism in a story that basically seeks to achieve its effects through a simple romancelike contrast between agreeable and disagreeable scenery, or a genuine attempt to fix the events that occur in it in a specific time and place.

It is difficult to make up one's mind about this because the chronological and the geographical details pull in opposite directions. While the chronology maneuvers the reader toward the naturalistic, historical end of the spectrum, the geography has the reverse effect. The place names in the novel are all fictional, and most of them don't even sound plausible. The town where Lantern Yard is situated is unnamed. Since it is "North" of Raveloe, and according to Dolly Winthrop it is "so long a journey" for Silas and Eppie to undertake, we can assume that it is to be identified with one of the Lancashire cotton towns in which both nonconformity and linen weavers would be commonplace by the 1780s. This is on the assumption that Raveloe, itself in the "rich central plain" of England, is to be located in the Warwickshire countryside around George Eliot's birthplace at South Farm, Arbury, near Nuneaton. The description we are given of its gently sloping hills, its woods and orchards leads us to believe this is so. In any case, George Eliot sets the principal scene of all of her novels of English provincial life in the West Midlands, though she never actually says so. Even Dorlcote Mill, which gives the impression of being situated in one of the flatter Eastern counties, was modeled on Arbury Mill, on the estate where her father had acted as land agent for the Newdigate family (St. Oggs was based on the market town of Gainsborough, in Lincolnshire). On the other hand Shepperton, in "Amos Barton," is described in terms similar to descriptions of the various northern towns of *Silas Marner*: "The roads are black with coal dust, the brick houses dingy with smoke; and at that time—the time of handloom weavers— every other cottage had a loom at its window" (*Scenes*, 23–24). This suggests that Silas might have traveled south into the Warwickshire countryside from the industrial towns north and northwest of Nuneaton, like the Black Country and Birmingham, or the Derbyshire-Nottingham-Leicester Midland triangle.

Interestingly, in *Silas Marner* we cannot solve the problem of geography by recourse to dialect. While the inhabitants of Raveloe give us plenty of opportunity to savor their regional dialect, we hear nothing at all of the dialect of the town. The Lantern Yard community speaks in a semi-biblical language that owes more to Puritan hymns and scriptures than to regional accent, judging from William Dane's conversation with Silas (we never hear any of the other members of the congregation speak). When Silas returns to the town with Eppie, we don't hear any of the townsfolk, not even the brushmaker, say anything. Silas speaks in a neutral accent, to be explained partly by his Lantern Yard training and partly, no doubt, from the central role he plays in the novel. I shall return to this last point about dialect when we come to look at the Lammeters.

Raveloe is located very specifically in time and only fairly specifically in place. The details of church going, dancing, baking, and weaving give the reader the impression that things are happening in a very real place, utterly familiar to its author, but not to be identified with any particular village or small town in rural Warwickshire in the 1790s and 1800s. George Eliot's novels are often discussed alongside Jane Austen's as developments of the social realism already present in the earlier writer's picture of life in the small villages and middling estates of southern England during that time. The odd thing about this is that when you compare George Eliot's Raveloe with Jane Austen's Highbury (in *Emma*), it is Highbury that seems the more authentic place, in spite of the fact that we are told so much less about its appearance and the things people do in it. It is a shock, however, at the opening of chapter 10 of *Emma* to find two of the characters talking about such mundane things as cheese and celery and beetroot, in a way it isn't at all a shock to find Dolly Winthrop dropping in at Silas's cottage with a lardy cake, or her son Aaron planning to cut slips of "stuff" like lavender and rosemary to replant in Eppie's garden. This goes to show that the impression of authenticity is not just a matter of the piling up of detail. But it isn't only that. Other places in George Eliot's fiction—Hayslope, St. Oggs, Middlemarch—are both authentic-seeming *and* full of the kind of detail we found in that particular part of *Emma* and throughout *Silas Marner*. The combination of lifelikeness and displacement that is so notable a feature of *Silas Marner* was obviously very deliberately contrived by George Eliot. It is an aspect of that blend of realism and romance discussed elsewhere in this book.

The boldest contrast between town and country occurs near the beginning of chapter 2:

And what could be more unlike that Lantern Yard world than the world in Raveloe?—orchards looking lazy with neglected plenty; the large church in the wide churchyard, which men gazed at lounging at their own doors in service-time; the purple-faced farmers jogging along the lanes or turning in at the Rainbow; homesteads, where men supped heavily and slept in the light of the evening hearth, and where women seemed to be laying up a stock of linen for the life to come. (63–64)

Here the impression of the "important-looking village" of chapter 1 is reinforced and even further exaggerated. The picture is more idyllic than realistic. The slightly earlier description of Silas rising in the deep morning quiet and looking out on the dewy brambles and rank, tufted grass sounds more like one of those scenes in Hardy's rural novels— Tess at Talbothays dairy, for example—where the reality of a working world strangely coexists with the symbolic representation of a pastoral Eden in which the recalcitrant detail of ordinary lives plays little part. Hardy, too, is often read as much as a social historian as a fabulist. Changes in agricultural practice in nineteenth-century Dorset count for as much in his work as the reform agitation of the same period does in George Eliot's. But in *Silas Marner* it is difficult to reconcile the idyll of Raveloe with the historical social facts of rural life during the French wars, described by one trustworthy historian as benefiting the landlord and large tenant farmers, and for a time checking the decline of the freehold yeoman and the copyhold peasant, but starving and pauperizing the common laborer.[21] Perhaps it is simply that the common laborer makes no appearance in Raveloe. All the drinkers in the Rainbow are craftsmen and tradesmen—butcher, farrier, wheelwright, publican, and tailor (who also happens to be parish clerk). Even the peasants who appear anonymously at the beginning of the novel—along with the shepherd, the pedlar, and the knife-grinder— don't put in an appearance later on. On the whole we don't get as much of an impression of the hard work that went into rural labor, let alone the insecure conditions—which, it is true, were different in the Midlands from what they were in the West Country at the time— as we do in Hardy.

Another gap is left in the fabric of village life by the absence of the poor law. Perhaps Raveloe is so small that charity to the poor is organized on an entirely ad hoc basis. This can't be entirely true because, after his money has been stolen, Silas is told by his neighbors that he is not worse off than other folk and that "if you was to be crippled, the parish 'ud give you a 'lowance" (130). Nobody seems to be poor in Raveloe. The lowest person on the social scale we meet there is probably Jem Rodney, the mole catcher. He seems to be able to manage well enough with a little poaching to supplement the income he gains from his profession. The same applies to the little we see of Tarley and Batherley. Outside Raveloe the poorest character in the novel, Molly Farren, is dressed in "dingy rags" not because of her inability to subsist on a barmaid's wages but because of her expensive addiction to opium. Raveloe does provide her with a pauper's burial. There isn't any suggestion, either, that anybody has been impoverished in the past. The conversation at the Rainbow ranges widely over a variety of subjects, but nobody who is gossiped about in the present or the past is represented there as poor. But we know that by the middle 1790s there was enough rural poverty in the land for magistrates in Berkshire to have invented what became known as the Speenhamland system, according to which low agricultural wages were supplemented with poor-law allowances that varied with the price of bread and the size of laborers' families. During the next 20 years or so, the years of *Silas Marner*, "Speenhamland," a recent English economic historian tells us, "became a shorthand expression for rural pauperization" far beyond Berkshire.[1] These are the circumstances George Crabbe writes about in his verse tales of the East Anglian poor in *The Parish Register* (1807) and *The Borough* (1810). His peasant Isaac Ashford dreads the workhouse, being "reluctant to be fed, / To join your poor, and eat the parish-bread."[2] He was lucky to die before the workhouse claimed him, but the same cannot be said for other inhabitants of the borough, and those in its poorer cottages and almshouses fared little better. It is difficult to believe that Warwickshire was so very different from Berkshire, Dorset, and Suffolk in the late eighteenth century that a village like Raveloe would be completely lacking in comparable figures, even if it were too small to boast similar institutions in which to house them.

It is a tribute to the extent to which the Victorians managed to soften and sentimentalize the poor in their fiction that the genuinely poor characters of Crabbe, of the Scots novelist John Galt, and of the first edition of Wordsworth's *Lyrical Ballads* failed to set a standard for how this sort of thing might be done. And it is not just a matter of the truthful representation of poverty, but of what Henry James calls "the grossly material life of agricultural England" in an essay on "The Novels of George Eliot" that singles out *Silas Marner* for the excellence of its portrayal of peasant life.[3] George Eliot had anticipated his comparison of her literary portraiture with the paintings of the Dutch masters of the seventeenth century. In what is probably her most famous nonfictional work, a review she contributed to the *Westminster* just a few years before she began writing novels, she asks, "What English artist even attempts to rival in truthfulness such studies of popular life as the pictures of Teniers or the ragged boys of Murillo?"[4] They were able to capture the "coarse apathy" and "suspicious selfishness" that are not to be found in the paintings of "heroic artisans" and "sentimental peasants" of contemporary Victorian artists like Holman Hunt. George Eliot thinks that English painters and writers should try to emulate these seventeenth-century artists:

> The slow gaze, in which no sense of beauty beams, no humour twinkles,—the slow utterance, and the heavy slouching walk, remind one rather of that melancholy animal the camel, than of the sturdy countryman, with striped stockings, red waistcoat and hat aside, who represents the traditional English peasant. ("German Life," 269)

It has been said that part of the Wordsworthian feel of *Silas Marner*—the scene at the Rainbow, for example—arises out of its lack of pictorial detail,[5] and this is true. The scene at the inn is created out of dialogue, not description. But the effect George Eliot creates through dialogue nonetheless bears comparison with the effects produced by the painters she admired, and her choice of Teniers and Murillo in the "German Life" review is significant. Teniers was a Flemish painter of the mid-seventeenth century who excelled at charming genre pictures, which were admired and collected by the aristocracy of his own day and of the following century. As early as 1775 we find Joseph Langhorne, in "The Country Justice," complimenting "Teniers' pencil" for its dexterity in portraying the faces of the poor in a moralized "picture of a winter day."[6] His paintings made this sort of appeal because of their anecdotal and picturesque representation of the life of the poor, often to be found drinking in alehouses like the Rainbow, and often including "people of quality" who are observing the actions of their inferiors in what has been described as a "mood of humorous condescension." His slightly older fellow countryman, Adrien Brouwer, is never mentioned by George Eliot. As I write this I am looking at reproduction of Brouwer's "Peasants Playing Cards in a Tavern" and Teniers's "The King Drinks"—both genre pieces set in a village tavern. Brouwer's peasants are just as George Eliot describes them in her review: heavy, slow, and slouching. Teniers' are much more decorous and well behaved. The effect of this preference of Teniers over Brouwer on English genre painting close to George Eliot's own day can be seen in the career of David Wilkie.[7] His small oil painting of "Peasants" in 1806 is in the tradition of Brouwer. But "The Blind Fiddler" of the following year has more in it of Teniers's charm and condescension, qualities carried forward and exaggerated in the paintings of the 1810s and 1820s.

The same is true of Murillo's Spanish peasant boys and girls of the same period. My catalogue describes his paintings, many of which were collected by Victorian connoisseurs, as displaying "a degree of conscious sentiment" not found in the work of his less popular contemporaries. "The Flower Girl," "Peasant Boy," "Boys eating Melons and Grapes" all show little boys and girls in torn, flimsy garments that nevertheless contrive to look clean and elegant.

This suggests that what George Eliot achieved in "peasant" scenes like the one in the Rainbow in *Silas Marner* was something less, certainly something other, than James insinuated in his essay and she herself anticipated in her review. In creating her sturdy "peasants"—

who are less sentimentalized than Teniers's but more refined than, according to her own prescription, they ought to be—she was not much helped by the execrable taste in art she happened to share with most of her readers.

The scene in the Rainbow has always been popular and usually receives more attention by critics of this novel than any other part. Leslie Stephen's commentary is still the best. In his day, it was already acceptable to describe the scene as "that famous conflict of rustic wits." Stephen, however, goes beyond complimenting George Eliot on her command of dialect and her ability to reproduce the play of attitudes and opinions among a fairly large group of clearly differentiated characters. He notices the way she pays tribute to the speakers' intelligence while fully taking into account the imperfect and distorted shape their halting expression of it takes:

> One can understand at a proper distance how a clever man comes to say a brilliant thing, and it is still more easy to understand how he can say a thoroughly silly thing, and, therefore, how he can simulate stupidity. But there is something mysterious in the power possessed by a few great humorists of converting themselves for the nonce into that peculiar condition of muddleheadedness dashed with grotesque flashes of common-sense which is natural to a half-educated mind. It is less difficult to draw either a perfect circle or a purely arbitrary line than to see what will be the proportion of the regular figure on some queer, lop-sided, and imperfectly-reflecting surface. And these quaint freaks of rustic intelligence seem to be rags and tatters of what would make wit and reason in a cultivated mind, but when put together in this grotesque kaleidoscopic confusion suggests, not simple nonsense, but a ludicrous parody of sense. To reproduce the effect, you have not simply to lower the activity of the reasoning machine, but to put it together on some essential plan, so as to bring out a new set of combinations distantly recalling the correct order. We require not a new defect of logic, but a new logical structure. (Carroll, 471)

No doubt a modern critic would fight shy of expressing views about what is or isn't "natural to a half-educated mind," and he would certainly stop short of "those quaint freaks of rustic intelligence."

Nevertheless, one sees what Stephen is getting at. Later he describes George Eliot as a silent guest in the Rainbow chimney corner. This guest "can at once sympathise and silently criticise; or rather, in the process of observation, carries on the two processes simultaneously by recognising at once the little oddities of the microcosm, and yet seeing them as merely an embodiment of the same thought and passions which present themselves on a larger scale elsewhere" (Carroll, 471–72). Any trace of snobbery or condescension attaching to this way of looking at the drinkers in the Rainbow disappears as soon as one notices that the same guest is present at other scenes in the novel where characters of greater elevation on the social scale are placed in the foreground. If the same combination of sympathy and criticism attaches to the Osgoods, the Lammeters, and the Casses as attaches here to the humble village tradesmen, a charge of snobbery or condescension cannot be made to stick.

An effective way of testing George Eliot on this point is to see whether she ostentatiously increases or decreases the level of sophistication of her own diction when she is reproducing theirs. One of the most odious practices of some of the English humorists is the habit of showing off their own and their readers' superiority to the characters they have invented by inflating their own vocabulary and complicating their own syntax while emphasizing the deflated and simply structured vocabulary and syntax of their characters' speech. Dickens is at his worst when he does this, and Scott and Thackeray are by no means free of it. George Eliot, though, is largely innocent in this respect. She is certainly guilty elsewhere of interrupting the racier dialogue of her characters with long-winded reflections and tiresome little polysyllabic parables and illustrations. But she doesn't do this at the expense of her characters, and she is very democratic about which of them she is prepared to interrupt. The language she uses to interrupt Squire Cass is not much different from the one she uses to interrupt Mr. Macey, and she doesn't do much of it to either of them. Nor does she condescend to her characters with the inverted snobbery of the American humorists (Ring Lardner and Damon Runyon, for instance) by ostentatiously adopting their own language *outside* the dialogue passages in their stories. The opening paragraph of chapter 6 avoids both of these extreme options and then makes way for the characters to take on almost the entire responsibility of managing the narrative. The nearest she comes to showing off her own superiority is where she has the butcher, Mr. Lundy, "slowly consider that he was giving a decided affirmative," but this is nothing compared with the treatment Dickens would have given him. Everywhere else in the chapter we are likely to take away the impression that George Eliot doesn't imagine herself to be superior to the characters and forgets about her sense of her own importance by attending so closely to theirs.

This is the secret of most kinds of successful storytelling: to give the impression that what you have to tell is so interesting that you are paying no attention at all to the way you are telling it. Leslie Stephen grasps this fact about the Rainbow scene when he comments on the way the characters appear to surprise even themselves with the aptness or accuracy of what they are saying. He writes about the landlord Mr. Snell's "quaint stumble into something surprising" (Carroll, 470) when he tells the farrier: "You're a doctor, I reckon, though you're only a cow-doctor; for a fly's a fly, though it may be a horse fly" (110). The same thing is true of Ben Winthrop's comparison between Mr. Tookey's inside being "nor better nor a hollow stalk" (98) for singing with, and, above all, at the end of chapter 6, Mr. Snell's wonderful argument about smelling ghosts and smelling cheeses. Many of these surprises take the form of comparisons, or similes, and the field from which the comparative terms are taken is invariably the round of country tasks and pastimes—bell ringing, reading a fingerpost, ridding a barn of vermin, as well as cutting stalks and making cheese—that the characters would be familiar with and that would have come naturally to mind. George Eliot falls into the same habit of expression, but her comparisons, with placing bets and attending funerals, are not as ostentatiously rustic. She is not pretending to be one of them. But she is not blatantly drawing attention to the fact that she is *not* one of them, either. This is the best way of making sure that they, and not the author, stay in the center of the picture. And that is what they do, in spite of the way that what they say has a habit of summoning to the reader's mind other matters with a wider reference.

It is not true that the conversation at the Rainbow has little connection with what is going on elsewhere. At first glance it might seem as if all that is happening is that we are being prepared for Silas's entrance after he has discovered the theft of his money and that in the process we hear something about Nancy Lammeter's family (we have already heard about Godfrey Cass's interest in Nancy, but she has not made an appearance yet). In fact there is a lot more to the chapter than this. The drinkers' conversation is a "ludicrous parody of sense." It is also a very subtle parody of themes that are clearly emerging in *Silas Marner* but that don't fully surface until the confrontation between Godfrey and Silas in chapter 19. In their clumsy way, the opinions expressed here about cows, choirs, wedding services, and ghosts have a bearing on how we are encouraged to interpret the conflict of interests between the Marners and the Casses.

The cow is the red Durham Mr. Lundy bought from Mr. Lammeter and that might or might not have been drenched, that is, dosed or purged, by Mr. Dowlas the farrier. Mr. Snell puts an end to the argument by agreeing with both of them. "Come, come," he says. "The truth lies atween you: you're both right and both wrong, as I allays say" (97). The next topic of conversation is Mr. Tookey's singing in the church choir. Ben Winthrop thinks it is awful. Tookey thinks it is more than passable. This time Mr. Macey adds fuel to the flames. He seizes on Tookey's expression of hope that there may be two opinions by telling him he is right: "There's allays two opinions; there's the 'pinion a man has of hisen, and there's the 'pinion other folks have on him. There be two 'pinions about a crooked bell, if the bell could hear itself" (98). But again the landlord acts as a peacemaker. Winthrop and Tookey are both right and both wrong: "I agree with Mr. Macey here, as there's two opinions; and if mine was asked, I should say they're both right. Tookey's right and Winthrop's right, and they've only got to split the difference and make themselves even" (99). Pacifying Mr. Macey over this carries the conversation on to the Lammeters, no doubt by way of a subliminal reversion to the subject of his cows. This introduces the business of the wedding service and the ghost. Macey's anxiety about Mr. Drumlow getting the words of the service wrong during old Mr. Lammeter's wedding to Miss Osgood is allayed by the parson himself. It's neither the meaning nor the words of the service that validate the marriage, but "it's the register does it," he says (102). And as for the ghost of Cliff's Holiday, it both exists and it doesn't exist, in a manner of speaking. Here again the landlord is the temporizing arbiter. It all depends on whether you've got a smell for ghosts: "I never see'd a ghost myself; but then I says to myself 'Very like I haven't got the smell for 'em.' I mean, putting a ghost for a smell, or else contrariwise. And so, I'm for holding with both sides; for, as I say, the truth lies between 'em" (105).

What all these arguments have in common is that they are resolved by being looked at in a way that removes the emphasis from the object being attended to and redirects it to the subject doing the attending. The resolution of the argument alters with the change in the point of view. This, at any rate, is Mr. Snell's opinion. But he would say that, wouldn't he, because as landlord of the Rainbow he doesn't want to lose the money of either of his customers through a mere difference of opinion. In point of fact Lundy's cow must actually have been bought from Mr. Lammeter, whether or not Dowlas had the drenching of it. It seems as if Tookey really is a poor singer, though he still has a claim to a position in the choir. The Lammeters' marriage *is* valid, in spite of the real error that crept into the religious ceremony. And if somebody who could smell a ghost and somebody who couldn't smell a ghost went together and stood all night by Warrens' stables, the probability is that neither of them would encounter Cliff's Holiday. Nevertheless, the absolute judgment hides a great deal of uncertainty that really does attach to the issue under discussion. And the same is true of events in the main plot. Silas deserves to keep Eppie with him as his daughter, and it is right that he should do so. But this simple statement hides a lot of other matters, concerning the rival claim of Godfrey and Nancy, that need to be included in the whole spectrum of our understanding of Eppie's position. They have to do with just those things that would have appeared on Mr. Drumlow's register (a marriage certificate between Godfrey and Molly Farren and a birth certificate for their child) and that old Mr. Macey further told him, "though there's folks nowadays know what happened afore they were born better nor they know their own business" (103).

Unbeknown to themselves, Mr. Snell, Mr. Macey, and the others are reciting in their own ways and in their own words the views George Eliot had read and sympathized with at the time of her bible studies and her editorship of the *Westminster Review*. The intersubjective nature of truth came directly from Spinoza's *Ethics*, which George Eliot had translated in the mid-1850s. Mr. Snell's speech about ghosts is almost a paraphrase, in the Midlands dialect, of a passage from George Eliot translation of Feuerbach's *The Essence of Christianity*, where the ability of the imagination to conceive of beings of a higher kind than man's own species corresponds with the powers of whoever it is that can smell both the cheese and ghosts that Mr. Snell can't smell at all. But the effect of our noticing these parallels is not to diminish the characters. They do not shrink into a shadow cast over them by their intellectual betters. Instead, the effect is to emphasize the coincidence of the same points of view among all sorts of people at all sorts of times. The men at the Rainbow share in a common human wisdom that issues from the lips of the grand and the humble alike, with no suggestion that the second is the pale reflection of the first, or, for that matter, that the first is the grandiose exaggeration of the second.

The scene at the Rainbow, including Silas's sudden and startling appearance during the conversation about ghosts that opens chapter 7, has been rightly admired. But admiration has deflected attention from the equally fine description of the investigation into the theft that preoccupies chapter 9. This contains a brilliant summary of the way the suspicions of the villagers alight on the figure of a traveling pedlar who visited the area a month before the crime took place. These suspicions are set in motion by the discovery of a tinderbox in the mud on the far side of the Stone-pit. The way the tinderbox becomes associated with the pedlar and the pedlar grows in the villagers' imaginations from a shadowy figure nobody can remember very clearly to a swarthy figure with a "look in his eye," a tinderbox in his hand, and big earrings "the shape of a young moon" in both his ears (114) is convincing. So is the occasion on which Godfrey calls at the Rainbow, adds his skeptical opinion to the rest of the conversation there, and is suspected by the villagers of going off to Tarley to throw cold water on the pedlar theory when in fact he is going to Batherley to see Bryce about Dunsey and Wildfire. This nicely carries us back from the theft of Silas's guineas to the quarrel between the Cass brothers over the secret of Molly Farren and the sale of the horse. George Eliot has earned plaudits for the ease with which she effects her transitions between the different strands of narrative in her later novels, but she does the same thing very discreetly here too. This is at least as important a narrative gift as the ability to rise to the big occasion and handle the big scene effectively, and we should not overlook it when examining George Eliot's literary skills in *Silas Marner*.

Christmas is the other big occasion on which we see the villagers of Raveloe together in a single place. But instead of meeting them in person, we look at the festivities obliquely, through the description of Mr. Macey's and Dolly Winthrop's visits to Silas. Each of them supplies us with a picture of Raveloe religion that is diametrically opposed to Lantern Yard's and is described in finer detail in the chapter 14 passage about Eppie's christening. Macey's practical charity extends to encouraging Silas to go to church once in a while and to arrange with Mr. Tookey, who has taken over his tailoring business, to make him a Sunday suit at a special price. Nothing sentimental about Mr. Macey. He will have to be paid, but not straight away, and not more than cost, perhaps. Lantern Yard would not approve of his casual references to Old Harry and the Wise Woman's charms, or his advice to Silas that he should "keep up your sperrits" because "there's windings i'things as may carry you to the far end o' the prayer-book afore you get back to 'em" (131–32). In fact George Eliot does try to diminish Macey by referring to his speech to Silas as a "discursive address," but Macey is irrepressible and goes on about the money just the same.

Dolly Winthrop, though, is a bit too good to be true. A single sentence of physical description brings to life what is otherwise a rather dull paragraph. The sentence tells us that she was "good-looking, fresh complexioned, having her lips always slightly screwed, as if she felt herself in a sick-room with the doctor or the clergyman present" (134). The paragraph stresses that she was a "comfortable woman," bringing into play a word that will continue to be associated with her person and her speech in all her later appearances. The trouble with Dolly is not that she is "comfortable" and helpful and sympathetic. Some people just are, and they have a right to exist in fiction as well as the liars and the hypocrites. But I never see those lips slightly screwed when she is speaking, and I never find that reference to her behavior in the sick room confirmed in her behavior toward Silas, her husband, or her children. As a matter of fact, George Eliot absentmindedly transfers Dolly's screwed-up lips to Mr. Macey at the Red House dance in the following chapter (160). The physical woman—her voice, gestures and expressions—tends to disappear behind the exemplary good sense of what she has to say. And what she has to say is straight out of Feuerbach in a less graphic and idiosyncratic way than was the case with her husband and his cronies in the Rainbow: things like "if there's any good to be got, we've need of it i' this world," and "if there's a good anywhere, we've need of it" (136). It is true that George Eliot interpolates a sentence to the effect that Dolly "did not lightly forsake a serviceable phrase," but we rather suspect that her creator didn't either. The most convincing thing about Dolly is her reference to the divinity as "Them." This was "her way of avoiding presumptuous familiarity" with the Almighty, which is plausible, but not made any the more winsome by being couched in those long Latin words that alert us to a hint of condescension so happily lacking in the scene at the inn.

Dolly is a more frequent churchgoer than most of Raveloe. At Christmas, though, the whole village attends the service, and the paragraph describing this gives as good an account as any of their attitude toward religion:

> But in Raveloe village the bells rang merrily, and the church was fuller than all through the rest of the year, with red faces among the abundant dark-green boughs—faces prepared for a longer service than usual by an odorous breakfast of toast and ale. Those green boughs, the hymn and anthem never heard but at Christmas—even the Athanasian Creed, which was discriminated from the others only as being longer and of exceptional virtue, since it was only

read on rare occasions—brought a vague exulting sense, for which the grown men could as little have found words as the children, that something great and mysterious had been done for them in heaven above and in earth below, which they were appropriating by their presence. And then the red faces made their way through the black biting frost to their own homes, feeling themselves free for the rest of the day to eat, drink, and be merry, and using that Christian freedom without diffidence. (141)

The emphasis on food and drink and music, the special hymn and anthem, the sense of a mystery that eludes systematization and the power of words to explain it, above all that "vague exulting sense" communicated by the presence of the abundant dark green boughs in the dead of winter—these are what Christmas and religion mean to Raveloe. The vagueness is important. It is the very opposite of what Lantern Yard wanted religion to be. And it is important too that the villagers feel they are "appropriating by their presence" whatever had been done for them in heaven above and on earth below. This is George Eliot's own religion of humanity in an Anglican guise, with the best impulses of her parishioners being reflected in the supernatural powers they have come together to worship. At this stage in the story Silas stays away from the service. Later, when he becomes a part of the village and its religious life, he will not have moved from a false religion to a true one. Instead, he will have moved from a true religion fanatically embraced and narrowly interpreted to a humanistic approach to life that discovers some of its most treasured symbols and ceremonies in the outward forms of the old faith. George Eliot admires this. It is religion on the Feuerbach principle. But as Dolly Winthrop shows—not in her behavior but in George Eliot's behavior toward her—it can be a little slack at the center. And, as I suggested earlier, it wasn't enough to save Silas from 15 years of misery and exclusion, any more than Lantern Yard was enough to prevent the coming into being of that misery and exclusion in the first place.

7

The Red House

Silas Marner is as much the story of Godfrey Cass's courtship of Nancy Lammeter as it is the story of Silas's loss of his guineas and discovery of Godfrey's child. The two plots are closely interconnected, but they appear to run on separate lines until chapter 13, when Silas bursts into the festivities at the Red House with news of Molly Farren's death. Dunstan's theft of the guineas occurs while Silas is elsewhere, and so this is the first time we encounter him in any form of association with the Casses or involved with anyone else in Raveloe. Even here Silas's involvement with Godfrey is handled perfunctorily, since the paternity of Molly's child is not known. It is only with the discovery of Dunsey's skeleton, 16 years later, that the principal characters of *Silas Marner* come together in anything resembling a dramatic conflict brought about by the exigencies of the plot.

Nevertheless, the close thematic parallels between the fortunes of the two men are not allowed to escape the reader's attention. The 15 years that elapse between Silas's arrival in Raveloe and the theft are closely paralleled by the 16 years that elapse between Godfrey's rejection of Eppie after her mother's death and the discovery of Dunsey's remains in the Stone-pit. Both of their histories during those years are histories of rejection of all that is best in themselves. Both of them are basically good men, naturally inclined to affirmative relationships with others. But each is persuaded by a combination of temperament and chance to reject the claims of affection represented in the one case by the village community at large, in the other by the child he has fathered. Godfrey's refusal to acknowledge Eppie as his own child provides the means whereby Silas is able to forge a connection with Raveloe that he has previously made no attempt to fashion. At the point where Godfrey fails to acknowledge Eppie and Silas exerts his own claim to her, there is an overlapping of their moral histories. Silas's estrangement from the community and from his own best self ends with the beginning of Godfrey's experience of the same thing. The childlessness of Godfrey's marriage to Nancy Lammeter, a coincidental punishment for his earlier sin against a child, is a consequence of that same type of estrangement from the claims of human kinship experienced by Silas in his solitary cottage during the preceding 15 years.

The ways in which their stories are told, though, are very different. They have to be different to express the respectively solitary and social conditions in which Silas and Godfrey conduct their lives. Unlike Silas, Godfrey is represented from the start as a man existing within a dense network of family and social relations. But we notice from the start that the vivacity of his social life increases and diminishes in conformity with whatever is or is not going on in his father's house. For this reason it is necessary to look at the Squire and the Red House before we can establish the main lines of development of Godfrey's fortunes. This is what George Eliot does. With both Silas and Godfrey she gives the reader a condensed history of the character's fortunes up to the time we meet him. But then Silas is left alone, or rather he leaves himself alone. This affects the way George Eliot describes his life between the accusation of theft at Lantern Yard and the arrival of Eppie at the Stone-pits. Godfrey, on the contrary, is rarely left alone, though he is often conceived of as being alone with his own thoughts even when at least one other character is present. For most of the time he is involved in conversation with someone or other at the Red House, and the sort of place the Red House is more than anything else influences the picture of him we take away with us.

We first step into the Red House immediately after reading about

Silas's mean, confined life near the Stone-pit at the end of chapter 2. It is with some relief, after the enveloping gloom of the cottage, that we hear at the opening of chapter 3 that "the greatest man in Raveloe was Squire Cass, who lived in the large red house with the handsome flight of stone steps in front and the high stables behind it, nearly opposite the church" (71). All seems light and air. The Squire's dwelling is seen at the center of "our old-fashioned country-life," "spread over a various surface, and breathed on variously by the multitudinous currents from the winds of heaven to the thought of men, which are for ever moving and crossing each other with incalculable results" (1). This emphasis on variety, difference, and uncertainty is in stark contrast with the simplicity, sameness, and predictability of Silas's life at the Stone-pits. So when the contrast is strengthened by remarks about undirected energy and Puritan earnestness, we can't help but be reminded of Silas's past and present. Raveloe, we are told, stands aloof from these things, and Squire Cass, with his boiling hams and his rounds of beef and barrels of ale, seems to stand for all that is most abundant and most festive about the village. This picture of plenty, completed with Mr. Osgood's feast at the Orchards—"hams and chines uncut, pork-pies with the scent of the fire in them, spun butter in all its freshness" (72)—seem to take all the sting out of the reference to the wider context of "glorious war-time" and a presentiment of ruin caused by "extravagant habits and bad husbandry" (71) with which the second long paragraph begins. And when we come to the New Year dance at chapter 11 the emphasis on the bustle and vitality of life at the Red House is resumed with even greater energy. Indeed the buzzing of conversation there—among the ladies dressing, the gentlemen come to fetch Solomon Macey with his fiddle from the hall, and the party from the Rainbow passing comment on the dancing and the music—increases the impression of the real satisfactions of a life lived communally, where everything is "as it should be" because "that was what everybody had been used to": "It was not thought of as an unbecoming levity for the old and middle-aged people to dance a little before sitting down to cards, but rather as part of their social duties. For what were these if not to be merry at appropriate times, interchanging visits and poultry with due frequency, paying each other old-established compliments in sound traditional phrases, passing well-tried personal jokes, urging your guests to eat and drink too much in your neighbour's house to show that you liked your cheer?" (158). We are given to understand that this was possible because the party comprised all "safe well-tested personalities" (156) who were known quantities both to themselves and their neighbors. Everything was as it was expected to be. Nothing was otherwise than it appeared.

Of course this is not really so. There are real festivity and true good fellowship among Raveloe's leading families, as there are among its humbler inhabitants. But there are misery and hardship too. Nowhere more so than at the Red House, as the very next part of chapter 3 soon lets us know. After all that beef and ale and spun butter, we discover that "the Squire's wife had died long ago, and the Red House was without that presence of the wife and mother that is the fountain of wholesome love and fear in parlour and kitchen" (72). The Squire spends a great deal of time at the Rainbow because he doesn't like to preside "under the shadow of his own dark wainscot." The same "dark wainscot" reappears at the opening of Godfrey's quarrel with Dunstan, the first scene to be set in the Squire's house. On this occasion it isn't only the fact that it is a dead time of the year, a late November afternoon, that accounts for the air of staleness and dejection that pervades the scene: "The fading grey light fell dimly on the walls decorated with guns, whips, and foxes' brushes, on coats and hats flung on the chairs, on tankards sending forth a scent of flat ale, and on a half-choked fire, with pipes propped up in the chimney-corners: signs of a domestic life destitute of any hallowing charm" (73). This is another of those genre scenes picked out with details of still lifes in the Dutch or Flemish manner, but without any of the animation or variety that customarily plays over the surface of those paintings. And sure enough, after our first close-up picture of Squire Cass, at the opening of chapter 9, his bearing is contrasted with the ordinary farmers' in the parish as not being that of a man who has "slouched" his way through life—precisely the word George Eliot used to describe the posture of the traditional English peasant in her essay on "The

Natural History of German Life." It soon becomes clear, though, that the fact that he doesn't slouch isn't entirely to be taken as a compliment to the Squire. His upright carriage is not by any means a point in his favor.

The Squire is "a tall, stout man of sixty, with a face in which the knit brow and rather hard glance seemed contradicted by the slack and feeble mouth" (120). He is among the best managed of all the subsidiary characters in *Silas Marner* because George Eliot is not in the least degree tempted to behave indulgently toward him. The preparatory work she has done on the village and the hall might be a temptation for the reader to expect a sentimental study. But that is just part of George Eliot's strategy for the representation of the varied strengths and weaknesses of the Raveloe community, and the Squire clearly accounts more for the weaknesses than the strengths. He combines a shabby, neglected appearance with an air of authority derived from the view he takes of his position and abilities. This impression of authority, we are told, could not survive a more scrupulous examination of his standing among the county families, for "the Squire had been used to parish homage all his life, used to the presupposition that his family, his tankard, and everything that was his were the oldest and best; and as he never associated with any gentry higher than himself, his opinion was not disturbed by comparison" (121).

The slipping in of those tankards among his family and possessions tells its own story. A little further down the page we find him ringing the bell for his ale while chastising Godfrey for having no more business than his own pleasure. In the late eighteenth century it would not have been surprising that a gentleman at breakfast should be drinking ale. But tea was by then an established breakfast drink. An anonymous poem of 1773 pictures the master of the house calling to the maid for "fragrant hysom tea" for breakfast, complete with tea rolls and butter and not—because it is summer—the "smoking muffin" he would enjoy later in the year.[1] This is a very different breakfast from the beef and beer of the contemporaneous Squire Cass. George Eliot never tells us in so many words, but it seems likely that the Squire is overfond of the bottle. We have already heard about his visits to the

Rainbow and have just overheard Godfrey reflecting on his irascibility. Later, at the dance, he is described as "noisily jovial" (152) and sets his "usual hospitable example of drinking before and after supper" (155). And Mr. Lammeter's "spare but healthy person" is contrasted with his own by virtue of its having "never been flushed by excess" (153). In any event his behavior has had a poor effect on his two elder sons. Before we ever meet them, we are told they had turned out "rather ill" according to the folk wisdom of Raveloe, which doesn't all that easily run to moral censure.

When we first see him in conversation with his son Godfrey, the harsh attitude he is going to take toward the death of Wildfire and the loss of the money he is expecting from Fowler are foreshadowed by an account of his treatment of his tenants. This *can* be indulgent, but it is often harsh. Godfrey has inherited the indulgence, which extends first and foremost to his own moral lapses. But he is incapable of applying the same unrelenting discipline to himself that his father applies to both his tenants and his children. George Eliot is very shrewd, and severe about the Squire's complacency in this respect. She tells us that his life was quite as idle as his sons', "but it was a fiction kept up by himself and his contemporaries in Raveloe that youth was exclusively the period of folly, and that their aged wisdom was constantly in a state of endurance mitigated by sarcasm" (121). While this is being said about him, the Squire is feeding Fleet, the deerhound, with "enough bits of beef," we are told, "to make a poor man's holiday dinner." The gesture show us all that is selfish and wrongheaded about him. But not only him. The sarcastic comment on "aged wisdom" among people in general, and among Cass's "contemporaries in Raveloe" in particular, enlarges the field of reference even where we feel that the lengths to which the Squire carries his folly has a more limited and a more specific application.

We are led to suppose, though, that these lapses in the Squire's character, uncorrected by the advice or persuasion of any close acquaintances or relations, have had a bad effect on the children. To a genetic inheritance of easy self-regard and easier irresponsibility has been added an upbringing tainted by the presence of just such defects in the character of the person who has assumed responsibility for it. George Eliot excels at tracing the details of inheritance in the behavior of the child. She is always good at discriminating between behavior that springs from inheritance and behavior that springs from training or upbringing. She understands that examining the interplay between these influences on a person's character might alter one's expectations about how that person will behave in a given situation. Godfrey and Dunstan have both suffered from the same defects of birth and education. Both have experienced that noxious combination of indulgence and severity, arbitrarily inflicted as their father's inclination or aversion dictated. But the weaknesses of their characters are expressed differently because they have responded to their father's personality with different degrees of respect, contempt, and indifference.

The picture we receive of them is partly a matter of what George Eliot wants us to understand about their characters. But it is partly also a matter of the different literary techniques she chooses to reveal them to us. Dunstan is bound to appear a simpler as well as a more wicked individual than Godfrey because George Eliot presents him more in terms of Victorian melodramatic conventions than she does his brother. He is not by any means just a figure of melodrama. But he owes more to the presence of such figures elsewhere in Victorian literature than Godfrey does. With Godfrey, George Eliot is more anxious to create a rounded picture of a complex though fairly shallow personality. Throughout her work we notice how she places side by side in the same plot figures whose characters and roles derive from different literary conventions, with varying degrees of dramatic, even melodramatic, presence and with varying degrees of psychological plausibility. Then she convinces us that they belong where she has found them, on the same plane of fictional narrative and in the same context of people, places, and events. Looking at Godfrey and Dunstan we have to ask ourselves how the melodramatic wickedness of the one can coexist with the psychologically plausible moral fallibility of the other; how the foreshortened history of Dunsey's blackmail, theft, and low cunning manages comfortably to occupy space in the same narrative with Godfrey's wavering uncertainties and fits and starts of conscience. Both the weakness and the wickedness originate in the Squire's inadequate endowment and upbringing of them. But the way they come over in the narrative has at least as much to do with variations in George Eliot's choice of literary conventions to describe them as it has with these more scientifically verifiable aspects of genetics and education.

Godfrey's first appearance (3) is delayed until we have heard about the Squire's position in Raveloe society, but it occurs before we have actually met him and been presented with a detailed sketch of his character. At this stage the Squire is associated with the general air of easy extravagance already being contrasted unfavorably with the more calculating generosity of the Lammeters. If Nancy were to marry Godfrey, so village gossip has it, it would be the saving of the old Squire, "for it was to be found that, notwithstanding his incomings, there were more holes in his pocket than the one where he put his own hand in" (73). Just before this we have heard the villagers' opinion of the two elder sons. Dunsey is "a spiteful jeering fellow" with a taste for gambling that "might turn out to be a sowing of something worse than wild oats" (73). His drinking reminds us of the Squire's visits to the Rainbow (mentioned in the same paragraph). (The Squire's tankards also make another appearance here, this time in association with the family monuments in the village church.) Godfrey has suffered from his father's neglect. There is anxiety lest he should "take to going along the same road with his brother, as he had seemed to do of late" (73). This is typical of George Eliot's method of introducing a character. The trick is to offer the reader a series of impressions of the characters taken by several more or less interested observers from within the text. Often she will start the process by bringing a character we already know into proximity with the main subject to register his impression of the person. Another good example is her introduction of the banker, Nicholas Bulstrode, in *Middlemarch*. She doesn't do this here, however. Instead she moves from general village opinion about the Squire to opinion from the same quarter about his two sons. That opinion turns out to be right about Dunstan, but only partly right about Godfrey, because the villagers don't know about Molly

Farren and therefore fail to understand what is behind there being "something wrong, more than common" (73).

We find out about what is wrong from the argument between Godfrey and Dunstan later in the chapter. The information is introduced in a rather stagey way, with Dunstan telling Godfrey what Godfrey already knows about the circumstances that have exposed him to blackmail. In fact much of the whole conversation has a stage-setting air. There is a lot of retrospective trawling for information the reader needs to know, and there is also a good deal of prolepsis regarding Molly's threats to spill the beans to the Squire, her likely death from laudanum, and the possible danger to Wildfire from Dunsey's partiality to drink. All of this is done without a trace of irony. It is melodramatic stuff, acceptable only because Dunsey—a character who is melodramatically conceived throughout—takes the initiative and has the most to say. In other circumstances Godfrey's contribution to the dialogue—"Hold your tongue about Miss Nancy, you fool, . . . else I'll throttle you"—would work against the conventions Eliot uses to present him most of the time.

The one ironic touch here, Godfrey's inability to go to Batherley himself because of the temptation to see Nancy Lammeter at Mr. Osgood's birthday dance, is also handled outside the melodramatic conventions. It arises out of the dialogue quite naturally and with considerable psychological plausibility. The fact remains, though, that the dialogue that follows Godfrey's appearance in the parlor and that looks as if it is there to tell us about *his* character and situation is actually conducted in a manner more suitable to the representation of Dunsey. It does tell us a lot about Godfrey—more than it tells us about Dunstan—but it doesn't dramatize his character very successfully, because what he says is couched so often in language more appropriate to his brother. We need to get behind the dialogue, behind the bluster that is the false expression of Godfrey's particular kind of weakness, to the inner recesses of a mind that is disclosing so little of itself as a result of this passive responsiveness to the pressure of another person's verbal habits. Later we are told that Godfrey's was a "pliant" nature. Here his pliancy has the effect of tailoring his individuality to his brother's mode of existence.

His own character emerges more forcefully in the analytical and discursive paragraphs that follow. Already a single long paragraph has told us as much about Godfrey's "natural irresolution and moral cowardice" as the dialogue around it has done. The paragraph opens with a description of his posture, with his back to the fire, and how he is "uneasily moving his fingers among the contents of his side-pockets, and looking at the floor" (76). Godfrey has a habit of looking at the floor when he is nonplussed. He does it again at the end of chapter 19 when Eppie has refused his offer of a home at the Red House with himself and Nancy: "His eyes were fixed on the floor, where he was moving the end of his stick" (234). This continuity of gesture adds conviction to the movement of George Eliot's characters from one period to another of their lives.

George Eliot's comment on irresolution and moral cowardice that follows opens a passage of more general reflection on Godfrey's position, which moves in and out of his own vision of it. At first, the seemingly impartial though severe judgment contained in that comment is prolonged in the words about his irritation at being provoked by Dunsey and his horror at "the miseries he must bring on himself by such a step," which "seemed more unendurable to him than the present evil" (77). That they only "seemed" to be more unendurable shows us that this is George Eliot's commentary on his reflections, not a description of the reflections themselves, as they passed through Godfrey's mind. But a little farther down the paragraph, those phrases that alert us to the mediating presence of the author—"from the near vision of that certainty," and the fanciful comparison with an uprooted tree—gradually disappear, and we feel that we are getting much closer to Godfrey than we were when George Eliot was inserting herself between his thoughts and our speculations. At "No! he would rather trust to casualties than his own resolve," we are right inside his head, thinking his thoughts with him. Not for long, though: "But his pride would not let him recommence the conversation" jerks us outside again. Godfrey would not use a word like "pride" about himself. That is George Eliot directing our moral attention to this failing in his character.

The point at which we enter Godfrey's mind and sense that we overhear him deliberating with his own conscience is the point at which one form of third-person narrative imperceptibly takes over from another. The technique is called the free indirect style, after a French phrase invented to describe what novelists like Flaubert were doing at roughly the same period in France.[2] It is the method whereby the grammar of third-person narrative is retained, but the tone, inflection, and vocabulary of the prose signal to the reader that what is being said is being said as the character whose thoughts are being described would have said it—that is, to himself rather than in the public language of dialogue, speech, or debate. Most of the time George Eliot's characters are not represented in this way, because her understanding of their moral foibles and lapses is far in excess of their own, and she wants to show this. From time to time she meets her match in psychological penetration, but only to score even more heavily in the ledger of moral judgment. Unlike the characters, she never imposes such judgments according to principles arrived at more by casuistical than by merely ingenious operations of conscience.

In *Silas Marner* there are no refined moralists or penetrating thinkers, so the author is always seen to be very much in control of her subject. Her comprehension of Godfrey's temperamental weaknesses, what she later calls "the old disposition to rely on chances which might be favourable to him" (119), is never in danger of getting entangled in the toils of his own mental deliberations. These deliberations are not complex, though they are subtle. But Godfrey doesn't register their subtlety. He allows himself to be taken in by the slipping and sliding of their passages across his conscience. George Eliot is forever drawing attention to "small indefinable influences" (80) that have escaped Godfrey's own notice. She points out the "insincerity" of his efforts to justify his conduct by recourse to inappropriate notions of "prudence." After recalling the scene where he manages to hide from his father the full scope of the Wildfire disaster, Godfrey notes how uneasy he was that "he had entangled himself still further in prevarication and deceit" (126). Always, one feels, George Eliot is a little bit ahead of her characters in arriving at an assessment of their moral failings. That is the impression we continue to receive of her treatment of Godfrey.

The analysis of these moral failings that follows Dunstan's departure moves still further away from Godfrey's own train of thought and substitutes for it an almost wholly detached narrator's viewpoint.

So detached is that viewpoint, so removed from the immediate fact of Godfrey's "ruminations on his present circumstances," that the circumstances George Eliot describes are almost certainly such as he would not himself ever have dreamed of considering. This breadth of treatment is much wider than his own could ever be, and it takes in much more matter than he could ever have been conscious of. Most of the three pages starting with "The lives of those rural fore-fathers" (79–80) onward form an essay on what George Eliot calls elsewhere "the doctrine of consequences." On this occasion it is adapted to the general purpose of underlining the pathos of ordinary lives, and only then the particular case of Godfrey Cass. Those rural forefathers remain obstinately plural:

> Calamities came to *them* too, and their early errors carried hard consequences: perhaps the love of some sweet maiden, the image of purity, order, and calm, had opened their eyes to the vision of a life in which the days would not seem too long, even without rioting; but the maiden was lost, and the vision passed away, and then what was left to them, especially when they had become too heavy for the hunt, or for carrying a gun over the furrows, but to drink and get merry, or to drink and get angry, so that they might be independent of variety, and say over again with eager emphasis the things they had said already any time that twelvemonth? Assuredly, among these flushed and dull-eyed men there were some whom—thanks to their native human-kindness—even riot could never drive into brutality; men who, when their cheeks were fresh, had felt the keen point of sorrow or remorse, had been pierced by the reeds they leaned on, or had lightly put their limbs in fetters from which no struggle could loose them; and under these sad circumstances, common to us all, their thoughts could find no resting-place outside the ever-trodden round of their own petty history. (79–80)

At last the application to Godfrey's situation is resumed: "That, at least, was the condition of Godfrey Cass in the six-and-twentieth year of his life." But it doesn't occur to us much at this moment to look forward to a hypothetical future for Godfrey, with his own particular gun and his own particular saddle, passing the rest of his days in such torpor. The reference is less specific, having to do with less clearly defined occasions of remorse, and with consequences having little to do with the one mentioned here. In fact Godfrey *doesn't* lose the maiden and the vision doesn't pass away. The paragraph about his affection for Nancy, however, returns us to Godfrey again. Even here, though, detail is sparse. We are told that the story of his affair with Molly Farren was one of "low passion, delusion, and waking from delusion, which needs not to be dragged from the privacy of Godfrey's bitter memory" (80). There is a hint of Dunstan's complicity in this affair, but it is quickly passed over. Then Nancy appears on the scene again. She is observed less as an individual person, with her own special traits of character, than as a representative of "the neatness, purity, and liberal orderliness of the Lammeter household" (81). At times she has the air of an allegorical figure out of *The Pilgrim's Progress*. She speaks with "the voice of the good angel" and would have drawn him into "paradise" out of a swamp (the Slough of Despond?) had he not "let himself be dragged back into mud and slime, in which it was useless to struggle" (81).

The effect of this is not to obscure Godfrey's personality with a cloud of discursive generalization, but to allow the discursive generalization to provide a firm underpinning for the particular case. By the time we have got to chapter 3 Godfrey stands out from the generalities just sufficiently to prepare us for the more detailed and humanizing treatment in both dialogue and description that will follow in his scenes with Nancy and the Squire. Then, too, the later, essaylike material on chance and consequence, the "evil principle" of "the orderly sequence by which the seed brings forth a crop after its kind" (127), will have accumulated a greater force in its retrospective application to Godfrey's conduct here and its prospective application to his future marriage with Nancy. In this last instance it is, of course, ironically phrased, since the whole point of that marriage is that it nearly founders on the seed bringing forth no crop at all.

For the time being we are prepared to take on trust the portrait of Godfrey as a man who has created for himself "a yoke . . . by wrong-doing" that "will breed hate in the kindliest nature" (82). We are prepared to accept George Eliot's word that "the good-humoured, affectionate-hearted Godfrey Cass was fast becoming a bitter man, visited by cruel wishes that seemed to enter, and depart, and enter again, like demons who had found in him a ready-garnished home" (82). Indeed, in other novels, the presence of these demons—created out of the consequences of a man's past misdeeds, and in their turn generating further consequences of an altogether darker and more deplorable character—often issues in sadistic cruelty or even murder, which we feel would be out of place in George Eliot's portrayal of Godfrey. Even so, Dunstan does die as an indirect result of Godfrey's moral turpitude, and his conscience about Eppie is aroused as a direct result of the discovery of Dunsey's skeleton. And Godfrey has willed Dunstan's death, even to the extent of making a warning sound like a threat of death (79); and he is deterred from flogging Dunsey "to within an inch of his life" only by fear "fed by feelings stronger even than his resentment" (78), which are never properly explained.

Incidentally, chapter 3 closes with an instructive vignette of Godfrey and his spaniel, Snuff, just as it begins with an equally instructive vignette of the Squire and his deerhound, Speed. Speed, you will remember, was being fed pieces of beef from the Squire's breakfast table, which was characteristic of the Squire and an exemplary comment on his inadequacies. Such is the case with Godfrey and his dog, too. Much of the discursive commentary on Godfrey's self-centerdness, bad temper, and general weakness of character is confirmed in his treatment of the dog: "Snuff, the brown spaniel, who had placed herself in front of him, and had been watching him for some time, now jumped up in impatience for the expected caress. But Godfrey thrust her away without looking at her, and left the room, followed humbly by the unresenting Snuff—perhaps because she saw no other career open to her" (82).

We fail to get very close to Nancy Lammeter's inner character because she is made so much of an example to us. But in her case, too, the dramatic deficiency is partly compensated by George Eliot's authoritative assessment of her moral strengths and weaknesses. Only partially, this time, because Nancy is a difficult character for George Eliot to criticize. True, she is pretty, and George Eliot often finds prettiness distasteful, usually discovering good moral reasons for chastising the pretty women in her books. Even here, the comparisons with her sister Priscilla don't by any means entirely work to Nancy's advantage. Nevertheless, she is mainly admired. She is a beacon to the unworthy and George Eliot always liked to see such beacons prominently situated and brightly lit. Her novels are full of such figures. They are the plaster saints referred to earlier. Other female versions of them that immediately spring to mind are Dinah Morris, the Methodist preacher, in *Adam Bede*, and Dorothea Casaubon, as seen through Will Ladislaw's eyes in the second half of *Middlemarch*. But Nancy's exemplary character is different from either of these because it is subjected to a great deal more inquisitiveness, even skepticism.

Before we meet Nancy, the emphasis placed on her family's "neatness" and "purity" and the extreme awe in which she is held by Godfrey—and, it appears, everybody else in Raveloe—doesn't bode at all well. I suspect most readers are relieved that she doesn't actually appear until more than half way through the novel, and even then only in the company of the excellent Miss Gunns, Miss Ladbrook (of the Old Pastures), and Mrs. Crackenthorp, "a small blinking woman, who fidgeted incessantly with her lace, ribbons, and gold chain, turning her head about and making subdued noises very much like a guinea-pig" (153). Better still, even when she is on her own, or when we are encouraged to ignore the press and bustle of the women surrounding her, Nancy shows occasional signs of imperfection. Though her thoughts "were always conducted with the propriety and moderation conspicuous in her manners" (146), she is nevertheless capable of remarking to herself that the Miss Gunns were "rather hard-featured than otherwise" and that "such very low dresses as they wore might have been attributed to vanity if their shoulders had been pretty" but that "being as they were, it was not reasonable to suppose that they showed their necks from a love of display, but rather from some obligation not inconsistent with sense and modesty" (146). And she is not above being catty when the occasion arises. One wonders whether her insistence that Priscilla wear the same silver-colored dress as she is wearing is entirely due to sisterly regard or whether she knows perfectly well that a sister looking "yalla as a daffodil" nicely sets off her own pale complexion. Also, there is something a bit finicky and extreme about sticking in "the very pins in her pincushion . . . after a pattern from which she was careful to allow no aberration" (147). There is something rebarbative about the "perfect, unvarying neatness" of her body. There is something more than dubious about the education she has received at Dame Tedman's school, which had made her "proud and exacting" in her constancy toward "baseless opinions" as well as "erring laws," though incapable of performing the simplest operations of mental arithmetic or coping with profane literature more advanced than mottoes about lambs and shepherdesses worked into her embroidery. All of these are very real indications of a rather juvenile severity, which is still much in evidence when we return to her in Part 2.

No doubt it would be going too far to suggest that Nancy's severity is as much responsible for spoiling Godfrey's happiness in his marriage as Molly Farren's shiftlessness—the reverse of these faults—was for spoiling his young manhood during the time he spent at home with the Squire. But there is some justification for making the comparison between the two women, and Nancy doesn't come out of it entirely unscathed. Otherwise her hands, rendered a little coarse by the butter making, and her country accent indicate something rather more practical and therefore admirable about her. And there can be no appeal against her possession of "the essential attributes of a lady—high veracity, delicate honour in her dealings, deference to others, and refined personal habits" (148). These are among the basic requirements of the Eliotic saint, and it is much to the author's credit that in the figure of Nancy they are convincingly shown to coexist with those other, less acceptable qualities, which are not just minor flaws stuck to the surface of her evident virtues, but the usually overlooked components of the virtues themselves. It is unusual to find George Eliot representing virtue as a compound. Vice is often a compound in her fiction, and part of the compound is often a sort of debased virtue. But virtue itself is normally elemental. The uncomfortable feeling we experience in Nancy's presence derives from our acknowledgment of the dark side that attaches to certain forms of virtue.

Another deliberate imperfection in George Eliot's treatment of the virtuous Nancy has to do with her accent. She *does* speak the Midlands dialect as a good farmer's daughter should, but *when* she speaks it we are not allowed to hear. The Miss Gunns think it is ignorant and vulgar to say "mate" for "meat," "'appen" for "perhaps," and "oss" for "horse." This is not quite the snobbery of a wine merchant's daughters from Lytherly slapping down the pretensions of a country girl who works in a dairy. It is almost certainly George Eliot's own attitude, reinforced by Victorian moral conventions. She lost no time getting rid of her own West Midlands accent (under the tutelage of Maria Lewis at the Miss Franklins' school in Coventry, when she was 11), and she never, after the Hetty Sorrel scenes in *Adam Bede* (which in any case she tidied up in the proofs), allowed her heroines, however rustic and however erring, to speak in dialect again. Nancy's own speech is standard English throughout, with the exception of the occasional *'ud* for *would* at moments of intense feeling. Elsewhere she behaves quite unlike her elder sister in always saying "of," for example, rather than "o'," which Priscilla does all the time. The Victorians didn't like their low-or middle-class heroes and heroines to sound boorish, and almost always gave them standard accents, however improbable the circumstances. *Oliver Twist* is the most celebrated and spectacular example, but even Mrs. Gaskell's working class heroines from the northern industrial towns are given only token regional accents, and when Charlotte Brontë brought out a new edition of *Wuthering Heights* after her sister Emily's death, she considerably toned down the Yorkshire dialect of its principal characters. Queenie Leavis adds a note on dialect to her addition of *Silas Marner*, but she ignores the Lammeter problem. A pity, because it does show something in George Eliot herself of that tendency toward neatness and severity that one is never entirely sure is an aspect of Nancy's saintliness or of her sinning—though most of the time one tends to favor the first over the second of these possibilities.

George Eliot's characterization of Dunstan is best considered outside the confines of his argument with Godfrey in chapter 3. We shall get the measure of him better at the Stone-pits than at the Red House. But in between the two he has a conversation with Bryce at the hunt that tells us a great deal not so much about Dunsey himself as about his ability to tell a tale, and this reflects interestingly on George Eliot's own powers as a storyteller. Bryce expresses surprise that Godfrey should have swapped Wildfire for Dunstan's own big-boned hack, and Dunsey has to persuade him that he has done so, all the same:

> "O, there was a little account between us," said Dunsey, carelessly, "and Wildfire made it even. I accommodated him by taking the horse, though it was against my will, for I'd got an itch for a mare o' Jortins—as rare a bit o' blood as ever you threw your leg across. But I shall keep Wildfire, now I've got him, though I'd a bid of a hundred and fifty for him the other day, from a man over at Flitton—he's buying for Lord Cromleck—a fellow with a cast in his eye, and a green waistcoat. But I mean to stick to Wildfire: I shan't get a better at a fence in a hurry. The mare's got more blood, but she's a bit too weak in the hind-quarters." (84)

In this little paragraph Dunsey uses many of the devices George Eliot also uses to enliven her narrative. The apparent carelessness with which he chooses his words is intended to prevent Bryce from noticing the direction Dunsey is trying to get him to follow. Under the guise of merely describing the horse, he is actually persuading Bryce to buy it. The "little account" between the brothers is left in the air. We know what it is all about because we have read the previous chapter. But Bryce simply accepts the evasive generality of the phrase because its particular reference doesn't appear to be important in the context of what he knows are the opening stages of a bargain being struck over the horse. Then there are the casually distributed proper names. In spite of the vagueness about the "account," Dunsey knows that in the right places specificity breeds conviction. Hence the pressing into service of Jortin, Flitton, and Lord Cromleck—two of which we are never to hear of again. The man from Flitton is not named because, in the middle of such a lot of naming, a single anonymous figure is plausible—especially if his physical appearance is sketched in so casually and economically: "a fellow with a cast in his eye, and a green waistcoat." All of these devices are used by George Eliot in other parts of the novel, especially in the crowded scenes at the Red House when the dance is taking place.

The dance at the Red House seems to arise quite naturally out of the descriptions of the seasonal festivities at Raveloe. But it follows immediately on the theft of Silas's money and is to be interrupted by news of Molly's journey through the snow and death on arrival at the cottage. In other words, the occasion is made to serve a strategic purpose and contribute toward the outcome of a story unfolding some distance beyond the boundaries of the Red House.

Here, too, characters we have not met before and will never meet again put in an appearance, which adds conviction and, indeed, population to the scene. This matter of population is more subtly dealt with than might at first appear. The Gunns, for example, are dramatized more vividly than the Ladbrooks, but both groups appear only once, in the bedroom, and disappear as named characters during the dance itself. The Squire's two younger boys are absent, except where one of them is needed to get something moving (Solomon Macey's fiddle playing on page 170). That one is called Bob, and we have heard of him once before (when Godfrey tells Dunstan that "Bob's my father's favourite" [75]), and we are to hear of him just once again (when he plays the hornpipe after the supper [170]). At other times he is not referred to at all, and his younger brother is always the merely anonymous fourth of Squire Cass's sons, never present in the narrative except to leave the breakfast room at the opening of chapter 9 so as to make a space for Godfrey and his father to quarrel. Servants, too, are rarely mentioned. Cox, Squire Cass's man of business, and Winthrop, his "managing-man," are the only people outside the family who are given a name, unless we are to suppose that Betty Jay, who "scented the boiling of Squire Cass's hams" (71) at the beginning of chapter 3, is a member of the household.

Proper servants materialize only at a later stage of the dance: "When the evening had advanced to this pitch of freedom and enjoyment, it was usual for the servants, the heavy duties of supper being well over, to get their share of amusement by coming to look on at the dancing; so that the back regions of the house were left in solitude" (170). They never appear again. At other times the Squire orders Godfrey to ring the bell for his ale, but we don't see anybody bring it to the breakfast table. A servant mentioned at the beginning of chapter 11 sounds as if she has arrived with the Lammeters and disappears immediately. All the other services performed in readiness for the dance are performed passively: the Miss Lammeters' bandboxes "had been deposited" on their arrival in the morning. These grammatical idiosyncrasies might sound trivial, but cumulatively they have the effect of linking together the minor divisions of the narrative with the least possible fuss and commotion. George Eliot has been careful not to achieve the effect of bustle and movement at the cost of too much crowding, too many named characters all competing for the reader's attention. The same applies to some incidents that have a bearing on the development of the plot but that we are not given an account of in the novel. The clearest example of this is Mrs. Osgood's birthday dance. Godfrey's presence there accounts for his inability to deal with the sale of Wildfire. But although the dance is mentioned four times (in chapters 3 and 5, and twice in chapter 8), we don't attend it with Godfrey, and we never find out who else went to it, apart from Nancy Lammeter.

An ability to hold the balance between a deficit and an excess in the narrative population is crucial to a writer's success in handling these social occasions. It is an art many more recent novelists have failed to learn from the Victorians, who tended on the whole to be very good at it. George Eliot admired Thackeray, whose *Vanity Fair*, published 10 years before her own first novel appeared, probably contains the highest proportion of such scenes, vividly and effervescently set before the reader, in the whole of Victorian fiction. But in its way George Eliot's performance in chapter 11 of *Silas Marner* is almost on a par with this achievement since, although it is much reduced in scale compared with Thackeray, it has to fit inside a much sparer and leaner fable than his and is therefore in far greater danger of upsetting the balance of the whole novel. In the middle of it all, George Eliot enlivens the scene with detail just as Dunsey did while talking to Bryce. Mr. Crackenthorp is introduced with the same sort of casual ease as the man with the cast in his eye and the green waistcoat: "He was not in the least lofty or aristocratic, but simply a merry-eyed, small-featured, grey-haired man, with his chin propped by an ample many-creased white neckcloth which seemed to predominate over every other point in his person, and somehow to impress its peculiar character on his remarks; so that to have considered his amenities apart from his cravat would have been a severe, and perhaps a dangerous, effort of abstraction" (152). The clause after the semicolon is a little insistent, perhaps, but the keynote of the cravat does its work and brings the little parson to life in a manner altogether effective and unassuming.

These are the methods of the novelist rather than the romancer; they are the means by which, to revert to Chase's words, "wide ranges of experience" are composed into "a moral centrality and equability of judgement" (Chase, 2). They play their part—along with the accurate dialogue, the controlled perspectives of the third-person narrative, the economical use of the free indirect style, and the occasional application of weighty, even ponderous, moral judgments—in giving the novel that air of solidity, conviction, and authority typical of its author's other, more spacious narratives. But we have still to account for the romance aspect of the tale, which is also very pronounced. Why does *Silas Marner* as a whole *not* read quite like George Eliot's other novels? What accounts for the impression of allegory and parable that we take away from it? To answer these questions we need to return to Silas himself, fled from Lantern Yard, but not yet a part of the community of Raveloe. We need to visit his cottage near the Stone-pits. And since we left Dunsey at the Red House, banging the door as he strode off for Batherley and about to pass by the Stone-pits both on his way there and back, who better to visit with than he? In any case, the melodramatic manner of his presentation makes him an ideal companion on such a journey. For melodrama is in many ways closer to romance than it is to novelistic verisimilitude, and, as we shall see, melodrama and romance have a contribution to make both to the psychological richness of George Eliot's study of guilt and redemption and to the symbolic status of the whole narrative.

8

The Stone-pit

Dunstan enters the cottage at the Stone-pit in the middle of a long paragraph tracing his fortunes from the moment Bryce agreed to the purchase of the horse to the moment he finds himself in front of the fire inside Silas's room (84–88). Events move rapidly within this paragraph. It contains an almost offhand account of the accident—"Dunstan, however, took a fence too many, and got his horse pierced with a hedge-stake"—a description of his return through the mist to Raveloe, and then of his arrival at Silas's cottage. At this point the narrative slows down, and the rest of the chapter, also a single long paragraph, tells us what went on in Dunstan's mind during the few minutes he spent looking round the room and then lifting the money-bags from the hole under the floorboards.

One thing that carries over from the first of these paragraphs to the second is Dunsey's whip. Or rather Godfrey's whip: Dunstan had taken it without Godfrey's permission "because it had a gold handle," on which the name *Godfrey Cass* was cut in deep letters. Along with his watch and seals this will turn out to be the means by which the skeleton in the Stone-pit is identified as Dunsey's in chapter 18. But for the moment the whip is closely associated with Dunsey. It is mentioned five times in as many pages. Dunsey raps the tops of his boots with it. He drags it along the hedgerow. He feels the ground with its handle to help him find his way through the fog. Right at the end of the chapter, before he "stepped forward into the darkness," he has difficulty grasping it along with one of the bags of guineas he has stolen. This intense focus of interest on the whip ensures that we keep on *seeing* Dunsey even when we are attending closely to what he is thinking. It also suggests something about Dunsey's character and reminds us that he has lost the horse he had borrowed to strike with it. But more than these things, it acts as a link between Dunstan, the gold, and Godfrey long before Godfrey is shamed into confessing his own errors regarding the golden-haired child, who, as we shall see, is closely associated with the gold Dunsey steals from Silas. When his gold-handled whip, with his name cut into it, is dredged from the Stone-pit, it is almost as if his own skeleton, not that of his brother, is buried there with it. And indeed a part of Godfrey has been dead ever since his brother disappeared, because his own child has been dead to him. In a sense he has swapped the golden guineas for the golden-haired child, and the gold-handled whip is a symbolic means of suggesting this to the reader some time before the events that explain it, in prosaic terms of plot and character, are recorded.

The light of the fire is used in a similar way. It is "the light gleaming through the chinks of Silas's shutters" that guides Dunsey to the cottage, just as it will guide Eppie in chapter 12. But with different results. While Eppie brings a true light to the cottage in the form of her golden curls to augment the light that guides her there, Dunsey takes away the light of Silas's world, false as it turns out to be, with the theft of his golden guineas. After the theft, Dunsey fears the light he had earlier sought: "He closed the door behind him immediately, that he might shut in the stream of light: a few steps would be enough to carry him beyond betrayal by the gleams from the shutter-chinks and the latch-hole" (89–90). That last phrase is wonderfully apt. Even such tiny glimmers of light might find him out. But the fact that he takes the steps he does to hide from the light damns him irrevocably. Again the use of symbolic imagery, arising so apparently artlessly from the surrounding circumstances, powerfully expresses themes of loss and reparation close to the heart of the novel's meaning.

In the middle of all this, though, the current of Dunsey's thoughts is described with a quite unsymbolic precision. First of all his eye is drawn to the contraption Silas has rigged up in front of the fire to roast a piece of pork. Only when Silas returns do we find out how this is supposed to work and why it has prevented him from taking his key to secure the door of his cottage. So we are as interested in it as Dunsey is, and we inspect it as thoroughly as if with his eyes. This means we are not greatly surprised when the question is asked, "The old staring simpleton had hot meat for his supper, then?" (88) and it turns out to be Dunsey's question, cast in the form of the third-person narrative. The contempt in the tone and in the choice of words to describe Silas is Dunsey's, but the point of view is as much ours as his. And this correspondence between the character's and the reader's point of view persists through a sequence of other questions until we reach the final question (for the time being), which is italicized: "*Who would know that anybody had come to take it* [the money] *away?*" I think it is here we disengage ourselves from Dunsey and register the absurdity of supposing that, just because Silas has left the cottage unlocked and his supper only partly cooked, he must have slipped into the Stone-pit and died. In fact, the preparation of the supper suggests otherwise. George Eliot sees that this is happening and pulls back from Dunsey's point of vantage, indicating that the question of the whereabouts of the money had taken entire possession of him.

Unfortunately, she chooses this occasion to slip in one of her wordy psychological generalizations, which turns out to be even wordier than usual: "A dull mind, once arriving at an inference that flatters a desire, is rarely able to retain the impression that the notion from which the inference started was purely problematic" (89). We needed to escape from Dunsey's mind at this moment, but not so as to be confined for the space of a couple of ungainly sentences in George Eliot's. With the remark about the three possible hiding places, however, we are back in the room, and the coincidence of Dunsey's and our own inspection of the room is resumed. The excitement of the search gets us over the little blip of "the stimulus of cupidity" and carries us effortlessly to the end of the chapter. On the whole, the movement in and out of Dunsey's mind, sharing his involvement and then distancing ourselves from it and becoming aware of the false assumptions he makes, works very well. And the elements of the scene that produce that extra symbolic effect work well with it too. They are never obtrusive. They never insist on their symbolic status. That is why they accumulate significance in the light of their reappearance or the appearance of objects and properties very much like them later in the story—whether at Eppie's arrival just a few weeks away or the draining of the Stone-pit after 16 years.

For readers of *Silas Marner*, Dunstan's whip and the light shining out of Silas's cottage have no insistently symbolic significance until George Eliot invests them with it at a later stage in the narrative. Nor do they have the same significance for Dunsey as they do for us. Indeed, it is Godfrey, later, at the Stone-pit, who attributes a meaning to the whip that confirms our own sense of its significance. Most of the time, though, the symbolic status of an object doesn't present itself so dramatically. It is something we simply take for granted. This is what Silas had done in his Lantern Yard days. He had known no other life. Consequently, he had invested in its paraphernalia—the order of the services, the prayers, the form of baptism—all symbolic values that created a sense of belonging, of having a meaning, of providing him with a purchase on the world around him. In this sense, symbolism is not at all mysterious. It is not a special faculty of the imagination, a sort of dreamlike thing to be associated with the Freudian subconscious or the hallucinatory landscapes of the surrealists. Indeed dreamlike is precisely what it isn't. On the contrary, deprivation of the power or efficiency of symbolism is what makes a man's life dreamlike and insubstantial, and this is precisely what we are told about Silas, on his arrival in Raveloe.

Typically, George Eliot allows the particular case to emerge slowly from a description of a general condition:

> Even people whose lives have been made various by learning, some-
> times find it hard to keep a fast hold on their habitual views of life,

on their faith in the Invisible, nay, on the sense that their past joys and sorrows are a real experience, when they are suddenly transported to a new land, where the beings around them know nothing of their history, and share none of their ideas—where their mother earth shows another lap, and human life has other forms than those on which their souls have been nourished. Minds that have been unhinged from their old faith and love, have perhaps sought this Lethean influence of exile, in which the past becomes dreamy because its symbols have all vanished, and the present too is dreamy because it is linked with no memories. But even *their* experience may hardly enable them thoroughly to imagine what was the effect on a simple weaver like Silas Marner, when he left his own country and people and came to settle in Raveloe. (62–63)

This is why George Eliot associates the wholeness and integrity of the individual so closely with the power of memory. What makes our selves whole and complete is the conjunction in them of our past and our present. Memory achieves this conjunction through the agency of symbolism, which can act upon the mind even where the symbolic object is absent. Physical exile, therefore, from the special circumstances of our past doesn't have to be accompanied by other, less tangible forms of exile—internal exile, which destroys personality by cutting away the *sense* of the past from the person who is living in the present. Godfrey Cass's willful rejection of his child and his inability to acknowledge her existence within the special circumstances of his marriage to Nancy Lammeter produce this effect of internal exile in his life. And earlier it looked as if the same would be true of Silas. The result of the lottery had produced in Silas a sense of estrangement from everything he had once valued. He knew he was innocent of the theft of the church funds. He also knew that according to everything he had once believed, he was pronounced guilty. So there were only two things he could do, either of which was intolerable. He could accept his guilt while knowing he was innocent, or he could maintain his innocence at the cost of rejecting everything else he had ever valued. The first chapter tells us that he made the second choice, and the second chapter shows us what were the immediate consequences of that choice, which had by now lasted for 15 years. "His life," we are told, "had reduced itself to the functions of weaving and hoarding" (68). What we are now allowed to see, but Silas, of necessity, is not, is that those activities themselves have a symbolic value. They are not only the plausible outcome of Silas's experiences at Lantern Yard. They are the most suitable, the most apt, means of expressing the psychological condition his experiences have created in him.

Silas has always been a weaver, so there can be nothing about weaving itself that explains the change in his moral condition after the flight from Lantern Yard. It all depends on how the activity of weaving is described. It is appropriate that Silas should take refuge from what George Eliot describes as "benumbing unbelief" by "getting into his loom" (62). Doing this meant that he was "working away as usual," but the verbal association of the man and the machine is very striking and anticipates the more elaborate comparison in chapter 2: "Strangely Marner's face and figure shrank and bent themselves into a constant mechanical relation to the objects of his life, so that he produced the same sort of impression as a handle or a crooked tube, which has no meaning standing apart" (69).

The reference to dreams that follows has a totally different value from the reference at the beginning of the chapter: "The prominent eyes that used to look trusting and dreamy, now looked as if they had been made to see only one kind of thing that was very small, like a tiny grain for which they hunted everywhere" (69). This is "dreamy" in the sense of making or discovering connections among all the apparently separate activities of life. The dreaminess referred to earlier is the opposite, of failing to make the connections and therefore being severed from a real and remembered past. Here the damage Silas is doing to himself by adapting so uncompromisingly to the demands of the machinery he uses is emphasized by the verbs *shrank* and *bent*. The appearance of age and decline that he exhibits is closely related to his association with the machine, in much the same way as the color of his skin, "withered and yellow," is associated with the gold that his work in the machine enables him to accumulate.

The other things Silas has become identified with are insects. Naturally, weaving brings spiders to mind, and spiders are the first insects with which Silas is compared: "He seemed to weave, like the spider, from pure impulse, without reflection" (64). And again, just a few lines further on, "all these immediate promptings helped, along with the weaving, to reduce his life to the unquestioning activity of a spinning insect." These references to insects always occur when George Eliot is emphasizing a lapse of memory. It is as if an insect is the least reflective living thing she can imagine, the creature least likely to look to the past in the midst of its frantic present activity. The spider weaves "without reflection." Mention of "a spinning insect" is followed by "He hated the thought of the past; there was nothing that called out his love and fellowship towards the strangers he had come amongst" (65). On the next page, the "insect-like existence into which his nature had shrunk" has deprived Silas of "a sense of unity between his past and present life." Later he is compared with a "plodding ant," "baffled by a blank like that which meets a plodding ant when the earth has broken away on its homeward path" (129). And when Eppie comes to reestablish the links between his past and present life, Silas ceases to be identified with spiders and beetles and ants and looks at the insects around him as separate creatures that provoke delight. His senses are reawakened "even to the old winter-flies that come crawling forth in the early spring sunshine, and warming him into joy" (184).

All spiders do is weave. They weave cobwebs. And here is another association with Silas. On two separate occasions in chapter 2, reference is made to the web Silas produces from his weaving. At first it is connected with the monotonous pattern he is making: "In this strange world, made a hopeless riddle to him, he might, if he had had a less intense nature, have sat weaving, weaving—looking towards the end of his pattern, or towards the end of his web"—might have done had it not been for the money that "marked off his weaving into periods" (68). The monotony of it all is stressed again on the next page, where "his eyes bent close down on the slow growth of sameness in the brownish web." George Eliot is fond of this word, not only in *Silas Marner*, but in her other novels too. She often uses it to emphasize the interconnectedness of people in society. At the beginning of the last chapter of *Middlemarch* she writes that "the fragment of a life, however typical, is not the sample of an even web,"[1] suggesting here that a single life might be viewed as connected together in the same way as the strands in a web of cloth. In the same novel the doctor, Tertius Lydgate, is searching for "certain primary webs or tissues" which will show "new connections and hitherto hidden facts of structure" (*Middlemarch*, 177).

These kinds of webs George Eliot clearly approves of. But it is easy to place the emphasis elsewhere, to stress the "evenness" of the web or the merely additive connection between one strand of it and another. Where this happens the value of what is woven sharply deteriorates. In Silas's case it takes the form of a life "narrowing and hardening itself more and more into a mere pulsation of desire and satisfaction that had no relation to any other being"—like a spider spinning a web, in other words. "The same sort of process," George Eliot tells us, "has perhaps been undergone by wiser men, when they have been cut off from faith and love" (68–69). So Silas's weaving of his web is just one humble version of a common error among George Eliot's characters. Here what is produced is squares of cloth and piles of guineas. There is no essential difference between this and, say, Edward Casaubon's uncompleted chapters of *The Key to all Mythologies* in *Middlemarch*. They are equally "cut off from faith and love" and therefore valueless. They are the "erudite research," "ingenious project," "well-knit theory" (69) George Eliot has in mind when she sums up the "processes" that are unlike Silas's in the scope of their ambition, but like them in the sterility of their inspiration.

"Every man's work, pursued steadily, tends in this way to become an end in itself" (64). Always in George Eliot this is a bad thing. All work, including the creation of works of art, serves an end beyond itself, and that end is a moral one. Nothing can fruitfully subsist "quite aloof from the life of belief and love" (65). Silas, though, is not an artist. The mechanical monotony of his weaving has nothing of the feeling of artistic creation about it. Since it is outside George Eliot's conception of the nature of creative and imaginative activity that it could ever be separated from some notion of moral usefulness, there is no reason why Silas's weaving, like Gwendolen's singing, or Casaubon's scholarship, or Lydgate's medical research, should not subserve the highest principles of human existence. When Silas was a member of the Lantern Yard community we were not told anything about his work, but we were told that the money he earned from it he valued because of the use to which it could be put: "he loved the *purpose* then" (65). What is done has a value not in itself but in its relation to the wider purposes of life. "But now, when all purpose was gone" (65), the activity of weaving itself becomes a primary value, providing as it does a mainly animal satisfaction for the hand and eye. Then, after the sale of Mrs. Osgood's table linen, the guineas he is paid produce the same effect, "like the weaving and the satisfaction of hunger" (65).

There is a significant difference, though, between the weaving and the accumulation of the guineas. This has to do with the intensity of Silas's satisfaction in the money, the almost sensual delight he takes in it. He "grasps" it "with a sense of fulfilled effort" that is expressed in terms of "desire." His life narrows around the iron pot in which his guineas keep rising "into a mere pulsation of desire and satisfaction that had no relation to any other being" (68). This is a hideous parody of those energies of the spirit that should turn outward to others to achieve their proper satisfaction. Indeed there is a sense that Silas's substitution of the gold for all of those memories—made bitter by his recent experience—that the gold has displaced can be explained in terms of George Eliot's recognition of the need men have to find in the world outside themselves a shape and a form for memory to cohere in. This explains the peculiar direction Silas's miserliness takes. Though it is not more sensual than the miserliness of Ben Jonson's Volpone, Molière's Harpagon, or Balzac's Grandet, the sensuous form of the accumulated piles of money is much more particular. Silas began to think the money was conscious of him, "as his loom was," and "he would on no account have exchanged those coins, which had become his familiars, for other coins with unknown faces" (68). He has not, then, lost his sense of a need for relationships with other human beings. He has simply lost his faith in real people along with his faith in religion. But he still collects faces, particular faces, which are not the same as any other faces even if they are only the faces of dead kings and queens stamped on coins.

More than this, it is not just other people he needs to associate with, but people he can imagine in some sort of familial relation to himself. The need to find a connection between a present and a future persists in his odd behavior toward the money, even if the connection with the past finds no parallel in it. For the coins are not just individuals, with individual faces on them. They are Silas's children. That is what must be meant by the comment at the end of chapter 2 that Silas "thought fondly of the guineas that were only half-earned by the work of his loom, as if they had been unborn children" (70). So the children are born when the guineas have been fully earned. Then they "were coming slowly through the coming years, through all his life, which spread far away before him, the end quite hidden by the countless days of weaving" (70). This, then, becomes the purpose, the end, for which the work is done. The money that Silas had thought of as the means to an end at Lantern Yard has become an end in itself—but an end, like the goal in raising children, that lies forever hidden in the prospect of future activity that will be required to bring it into being. Of course this is a terrible misconception, this banal substitution of the addition of one coin to another for the guidance and nurture of a living person. But the origin of the desire in Silas's innermost being shows that he is not quite lost to himself and his fellow men. What he loves in the money is what he will be able to love again in the world at large. Even the imagery used to describe it is the imagery he was familiar with in the old days. It may be that the past he has shrunk from is "like a rivulet that has sunk far down from the grassy fringes of its old breadth into a little shivering thread" (70), but the way he looks at the guineas is equally palpably expressed through images of water and replenishment: "He spread them [the coins] out in heaps and *bathed* his hands in them" (70). "How the guineas shone as they came *pouring* out of their dark leather mouths" (70). It is almost as if he is being baptized in the money, as if the familiar images of life and hope persist even where what they stand for is being rejected and denied. These images of children and baptism and shining light are not used ironically by George Eliot. They are deployed with a straightforward moral force to prepare the reader for Silas's entirely plausible, and profound, transformation when Eppie takes the place of the gold, but in doing so does not take the place of everything the gold has meant to him.

Immediately after the passages in chapter 2 about the weaving and the hoarding of the money, George Eliot adds a paragraph to illustrate how incomplete Silas's decline has been. The first passage ends with a pessimistic summing up of his condition that sounds final: "Thought was arrested by utter bewilderment, now its old narrow pathway was closed, and affection seemed to have died under the bruise that had fallen on its keenest nerves" (65). But the hopelessness of "*utter* [italics added] bewilderment" is slightly modified by "*seemed* [italics added] to have died." Then there is the business of Mrs. Osgood's table linen. This exacerbates the problem by introducing the financial issue. It ends with a description of Silas walking home across the fields and watching the money in his hand grow brighter in the gathering gloom. Even so, the illustration that follows is of Silas's curing Sally Oates's heart disease, which made him feel for the first time since he arrived in the village "a sense of unity between his past and present life" (66). But this comes to nothing. The villagers' superstition and disbelief combine to drive Silas in on himself again. "Thus it came to pass that his moment of pity towards Sally Oates, which had given him a transient sense of brotherhood, heightened the repulsion between him and his neighbours, and made his isolation more complete" (67). There follow the paragraphs about the coins becoming his familiars, and his body shrinking and bending itself into a constant mechanical relation to the objects of his life. And after it, the description of the brown earthenware pot he breaks after stumbling against a stile. Each of these illustrations is introduced with the most primitive narrative tag: "About this time an incident happened . . ."; "Yet even at this stage of withering a little incident happened. . . ." The movement from condensed to more dramatic narrative is clearly signaled, but the upshot of it all is that we remain somewhat at a distance from Silas. From time to time we home in on his thoughts as they occur, with an occasional emotional repetition—"weaving, weaving"—or with a close and interested attention to detail—the image of the coins slipping through Silas's hands, where the common pronoun "them" [the coins] turns up over and over again (compare with Daniel Defoe's description of the infected purse in *A Journal of the Plague Year*). When Silas next appears, in chapter 5, after the account of Dunsey's's theft of the money, the treatment is more sharply dramatic. His discovery of the theft is handled very differently from his actions since the "trial" at Lantern Yard. There is even something that could be described as cinematic in the way his movements and gestures are made to impress upon us his desperation.

First, though, George Eliot must outline the general condition influencing his behavior. No sooner has Silas appeared, with a sack on his shoulders and a lantern in his hand, than his earlier absence from the cottage is explained in a little essay about the sense of security and presentiment of change. There is no harm done, however, because we have not had time to get close to Silas at this early stage, and the essay does convincingly explain why he left the door unlocked. Also the explanation leads very smoothly into an account of his complicated arrangements over the roast pork, moving easily from his anticipation of a good dinner to a description of how he had assembled the string, the key, and the hanger to make sure he would get it. As a result, we return to Silas with a succession of rhetorical questions ringing in our ears at the moment he arrives back at the cottage: "What thief would find his way to the Stone-pits on such a night as this? . . ." (91). These are the questions Silas asked himself before he went out and that might still have been drifting through his mind on his way back. They are cast in the present at this point in the narrative but are not present in Silas's mind as we hear them being asked. George Eliot explains that "these questions were not distinctly present in Silas's mind; they merely serve to represent the vaguely-felt foundation of his freedom from anxiety" (91). The author is interpreting the character's state of mind through a condensed narrative of the workings of that mind cast in the form of a series of present-tense questions. It is a peculiar hybrid of detached and dramatized description. As such it works very well to shift the reader's attention easily from the retrospective material at the opening of the chapter to the more dramatic narrative that follows.

Silas's discovery of the theft is one of the most powerful pieces of writing in the whole of George Eliot's work. It begins unambitiously, with a simple account of Silas's movements around the room: first with his eyes, then his feet. The particularity of the description, later to grow into an intense concentration on the minutiae of the scene, starts to register when we are told how the lantern and the sack, thrown aside as he puts out his lantern, have the effect of "merging the marks of Dunstan's feet on the sand in the marks of his own nailed boots" (91–92). Again we see Dunsey pacing about the room searching for the gold, and we know Silas will do the same, when he realizes that there will be no occasion to resume "the agreeable business of tending the meat and warming himself at the same time" (92). He always likes to inspect his guineas before he eats. The more discursive sentences of the next paragraph remind us of his enslavement to the gold, and the imperfect tense of the last of them is deliberately cast in the form of the past definite to give an edge of immediacy, and what we know will be an immediate horror, to what he is about to discover: "His gold, as he *hung* over it and *saw* it grow, gathered his power of loving together in a hard isolation like its own" (92).

The strength of the writing that follows lies in the accuracy with which George Eliot traces Silas's movements and responses, and the clarity of the picture she sets before us. Each stage or phase in Silas's discovery of the theft is utterly convincing: first the violent physical response to the sight of the empty hole, then the combination of disbelief and terror; the trembling search around the hole with his hands, the candle falling, the dizzy spell; the panicky exploration of the rest of the room; the cry that relieves him of "the first maddening pressure of the truth." And then, just as one would expect, "he turned, and tottered towards his loom, and got into the seat where he worked, instinctively seeking this as the strongest assurance of reality" (93). Each of us at some time or other have had the experience of losing something he must get back, must have, that mustn't really be lost because how could it have been? These are precisely the thoughts Silas has running through his head. And they are in the right order, too. Silas's retirement into the loom is a function of his particular character. But the tangible assurance of reality it provides him brings the truth of it home to all of us. All of this is done with immense restraint. The generalizations from the particular case are few, just two of them. The first is brief, almost proverbial: "A man falling into dark waters seeks a momentary footing even on sliding stones" (93). Again a scene from *The Pilgrim's Progress* flashes across our minds. The second is longer and less metaphorical, about the expectation of impossibilities that is distinct from madness only because it can be dissipated by external fact. This is a little bit wordy, but is otherwise a very precise statement and is minutely adapted to Silas's state of mind. The rest of the chapter is description, with no generalization at all.

It is not only the dark waters and the sliding stones that return us to the world of parable and *The Pilgrim's Progress*. There is the "cry of desolation" too. Surely this is a reminder of Bunyan's allegory, where Christian "brake out with a lamentable cry; saying, 'What shall I do?' "? (Bunyan, 39). The point George Eliot is making, however, is that Silas's desolation is different from Christian's because the missing gold is not to be equated with what Christian has read in the book he holds in front of him. Both will be saved, but one because he holds firm to the object that has prompted the scream, the other because he is reconciled to his loss of it. In any case, Silas's scream has an immediate therapeutic effect. There is no Evangelist to help him. Instead, there is just a temporary physical relief. And instead of fleeing from his house, his wife, and his children, as Christian does, Silas will remain in his house, and what is to be accounted "his" child will come to him. The flight away from relationship preceded the loss of the guineas by at least 15 years. In George Eliot's secular fable, a man's soul is not gained, but lost, by separation from his fellows; and the event that has provoked his cry will eventually, by a roundabout route, return him to the City of erring humanity, not thrust him further away from it.

There can be no more evident sign that the City is indeed erring than the opening to the next paragraph: "And now that all the false hopes had vanished, and the first shock of certainty was past, the idea of a thief began to present itself, and he entertained it eagerly, because a thief might be caught and made to restore the gold" (91). The wish is father to the thought. This is exactly the way Dunsey thought when he entered the cottage. He too imagined that circumstances were what he wanted them to be. The door was unlocked, Silas was not there, it was foggy outside and easy to lose your way and miss your step. Therefore Silas must be dead and Dunsey can carry off the gold, if he can find it, without fear of consequences. But he was wrong. Silas was alive and well and on his way back to the cottage. It is Dunsey who will fall into the Stone-pit and drown. So, here. Silas grabs at the idea of a thief because a thief is something tangible that can be caught and made to deliver up the money he has stolen. He doesn't think this because it is especially likely, because it is the best explanation for what has happened. It may well be that this aspect of Silas's deliberations wouldn't have struck us as all that strange if George Eliot hadn't drawn it to our attention by making Silas dwell on it so emphatically. We would have asked ourselves what other explanation can there be, once it has been established that the money really isn't in the cottage? But that is not the way Silas is used to thinking. He had enough respect for common reality at Lantern Yard to rebel against a superstitious judgment he knew to be wrong. But he *is* superstitious. He does still think in terms of "a cruel power no hand could reach" (94), like the one that governed the outcome of the lottery. This is the "vaguer dread" that is very real to Silas. He sets it aside not because it is implausible but because it is too awful to contemplate. It is for this reason that he "fixed his mind with struggling effort on the robber with hands, who could be reached by hands" (94). That is very powerfully expressed. The physicality of it and the almost biblical ring of repetition of the phrase about hands emphasize Silas's desperation and prepare the way for the narrowing of his wish fulfillment into the shape of Jem Rodney, "a known poacher," a disreputable individual who has made jokes about Silas's money in the past and who is therefore the obvious culprit.

With the emergence of this figure in Silas's mind the hallucinatory details of the room—the bricks, the door, the loom—begin to fade, and with them there fades too the sense of his stifling obsession. The faces of the "great people of the village" follow Jem Rodney's across his mind, and as he rushes out into the night we are returned to the world of routine, of the ordinary, of the commonplace. By the time Silas has appeared like a ghost in the kitchen of the Rainbow we have been there for the space of a whole chapter, and his "strange unearthly eyes" strike us as violently as they do the rest of the company. The interior drama of Silas's mind has given way to something less intense and less disturbing, though every bit as vivid. We can well understand how it is that "this strangely novel situation of opening his trouble to his Raveloe neighbours, of sitting in the warmth of a hearth not his own" should have at least a temporary influence on Silas "in spite of his passionate preoccupation with his loss" (108). But it will only be temporary. The warmth and promise of help will have to come to his own hearth before its influence will be permanent. The way this happens will be as powerfully represented as the loss of his gold was, but not in the same way. Here, the psychological drama of the discovery of the theft, and the more extrovert drama of the scene at the Rainbow, give way to something not dramatic at all, but told more in the manner of a folktale or fairy story. The suggestion of parable and allegory that is strong in the first images we see of Silas and the last we see of Dunsey has become more closely worked into the texture of the narrative. As this happens it brings out other aspects of romance, as opposed to realistic description, that have been hovering in the background of the story so far.

Few readers would claim that Eppie was one of the triumphs of this novel. The 16-year-old girl one finds simpering about flowers, "frisking" "roguishly" with Snap the dog and Puss the cat, and making things bright and clean and tidy for when Aunt Dolly comes to visit is not as easy to love as her winning ways suggest. In coming to appreciate the impact she makes on Silas's life, we need to put as far out of our minds as possible the paragon of innocence who is such a tribute to Silas's upbringing, and concentrate on the toddler Silas discovers in the cottage at the end of chapter 12. Even here the omens are not entirely propitious. Victorian novels are full of unmarried mothers (though Molly *is* married) stumbling about the country and depositing unwanted babies on somebody or other's doorstep. The opening chapter of *Oliver Twist* is the most famous of these. And we have been warned that this particular infant is intended to be the bearer of the "Unseen Love" that will care for Silas (65) and the "phantom of delight to still the poor soul's craving" (129). It is a heavy burden for any child to bear. But there is a great deal of difference between the treatment of the child before its mother's death and after it. Before her death, the child is viewed by us directly, first of all clutched to its mother's bosom, then toddling through the snow to Silas's door. The inadequacy of the writing here can be measured by the number of times Eppie is described as being "little." It isn't just that she is identified as "the little one," which is no more or less than a synonym for "infant." In a single paragraph she also utters "a little peevish cry," has a "little head," a "little golden head" in fact, at the back of which dangles a "queer little bonnet," and holds out both a "little hand" outside the door and two "tiny hands" inside it (165–66). This constitutes a direct assault on the reader's powers of feeling, and when we speak of the sentimentality of Victorian fiction it is this transparent substitution of a call to sympathy in place of a clear and unobstructed picture of the facts. It will not do to minimize the extent of George Eliot's failure here. But we need to discriminate between this failure and her success in communicating the profound effect Silas's discovery of the baby has on him.

After Eppie has fallen asleep on the old sack by the hearth, the narrative returns to Silas, showing why he had failed to notice her arrival at the cottage. For a second time in the plot, the first since the theft of the church funds, he is the victim of a cataleptic trance: "He was arrested, as he had been already since his loss, by the invisible wand of catalepsy, and stood like a graven image, with wide but sightless eyes, holding open his door, powerless to resist either the good or evil that might enter there" (167). The link between the evil that occurred at Lantern Yard and the good or evil that is about to occur here by the Stone-pit is boldly established, and the reversion to romance narrative is signaled by the image of an "invisible wand." When Silas comes out of his trance and turns his attention to what lies inside the cottage, the manner of fairy-tale romance is continued, but instead of looking directly at Silas and the child, as we did at the child and its mother, we encounter the child as if for the first time through Silas's eyes. His vision is "blurred," and what he sees, because it was in his mind immediately before he went into the trance, is his gold lit up by the uncertain glimmer of the fire: "Gold!—his own gold— brought back to him as mysteriously as it had been taken away!" (167). And then, at last, when he manages to stretch out his hand to "grasp" the "treasure," it is transformed from something "hard" and "resistant" to something "soft" and "warm" instead. We experience this, as Silas does, not as a disappointment but as a relief for two reasons: first, because of the sensory preference we are all likely to have for warmth and softness over cold and hardness; and, second, because of the way in which the anonymous sleeping child is intuitively identified by Silas as his little sister, of whom we have already heard, and who, in this surrogate form, releases the floodgates of memory and unblocks the barrier between the past and present. This explains why Silas undergoes a sort of collapse "under the double presence of an inexplicable surprise and a hurrying influx of memories" (168). It also explains why Eppie is perceived simply and unfussily as a "child" and is described as little only because she reminds him of his little (younger) sister. Only once in the three, mainly long, paragraphs describing Silas's vision of Eppie is any one part of her described as "little," and that is "the marks made by the little feet in the virgin snow" (169). They have to be "little" to explain Silas's difficulty in tracing them to the dead woman.

Silas realizes that the image before him is one of a golden-haired child, and not of actual gold, through the sense of touch. "He leaned forward—and stretched forth his hand; but instead of hard coin with the familiar resisting outline, his fingers encountered soft warm curls" (167). This, too, gathers Silas and the child into a world of legend and fairy tale. It is a version of the story of King Midas of Phrygia, who possessed the gift of turning all that he touched to gold. In Hawthorne's version of the story, which George Eliot had probably read in *Tanglewood Tales* (published in 1853), the king has a daughter called Marygold, who is also turned to gold when she runs to give him a kiss. Just before Eppie's arrival, Silas had been standing at his door "as if he thought his money might be somehow coming back to him" (166). But what actually comes back to him is the habit of affection he had lost before he came to Raveloe, possibly soon after his sister's death. Instead of the girl turning into gold, the gold turns into a girl, a girl who calls forth all the desperate love he had earlier lavished on his sister. All through the story after this incident, the symbolic exchange of the gold for the child is insisted on. "The money's gone," Silas says to Dolly when she offers him a bundle of children's clothes. "I don't know where, and this [Eppie] is come from I don't know where" (179). And again, "he could only have said that the child was come instead of the gold—that the gold had turned into the child" (180). This is only one of many references to the transformation of the guineas—that were once, if only fancifully, described as unborn children—into an actual, living child.

The Midas story is one of several myths and legends that readers have discovered underpinning the romance narrative of *Silas Marner*. Another is the story of Rumpelstiltskin (not, in my view, much of a parallel, in spite of the fact that Rumpelstiltskin was a weaver and also that Grimm's fairy tales were translated into English in 1823, just in time for George Eliot to enjoy reading them or having them read to her as a small child). Even the Norns of Norse mythology have been pressed into service. But a story that is clearly discernible beneath the detail of Silas's relationship with Eppie is that of Shakespeare's *The Winter's Tale*. All of the relevant features of the story are displaced and redistributed, but here also we have a tale of the loss and restoration of a child, the association of the child with a pile of gold, the upbringing of a wealthy man's daughter in the humble setting of a rustic home, and the love of an adopted child for an adoptive father. Like Perdita, Eppie "was not quite a common village maiden, but had a touch of refinement and fervour which came from no other teaching than that of tenderly-nurtured unvitiated feeling" (206). Even the choice of words is similar. Later, Godfrey tells Silas that "she doesn't look like a strapping girl come from working parents" (228). The important thing about this isn't that there is a specific source in *The Winter's Tale*, but that the things that make this play the most fairy-tale-like and romantic of Shakespeare's works produce a similar effect in *Silas Marner*. They confirm the point George Eliot seemed to be making when she confessed to John Blackwood that it was "a story which came across my other plans by a sudden inspiration" (Draper, 37), or, in a slightly later letter to the same correspondent, that "it came to me first of all, quite suddenly, as a sort of legendary tale" (Draper, 38).

Another very precise parallel with *The Winter's Tale* is the lapse of 16 years between the abandonment of the child and the discovery of her true parentage. This is not as remarkable as at first it sounds, because the progress of the story demands that in each case the discovery should occur at the same time as the grown-up child is ready to marry. Also, in both the play and the novel the 16 years pass with little or no description of the child's upbringing. This is done more startlingly in the play, where Time comes onto the stage to tell the audience that 16 years have passed. George Eliot is a little less abrupt. She inserts a chapter (chapter 14) that carries the reader through those 16 years by alternating general statements about how Silas fosters Eppie and how he grows closer to Raveloe through the care he takes of her with a couple of scenes—Dolly over the christening and Eppie alone over the boot and the coal hole—that briefly illuminate his difficulties. The scenes work effectively enough and avoid most of the familiar hazards of emotional indulgence and sentimentality, but it is the condensed descriptive writing that does most to convince the reader of Silas's regeneration. This is especially true of the paragraph that connects the scenes of the christening and of the boot and coal hole, in which George Eliot explains how "the child created fresh links between his life and the lives from which he had hitherto shrunk continually into narrow isolation":

> Unlike the gold which needed nothing, and must be worshipped in close-locked solitude—which was hidden away from the daylight, was deaf to the song of birds, and started to no human tones— Eppie was a creature of endless claims and ever-growing desires, seeking and loving sunshine, and living sound, and living movements; making trial of everything, with trust in new joy, and stirring the human kindness in all eyes that looked on her. The gold had

kept his thoughts in an ever-repeated circle, leading to nothing beyond itself; but Eppie was an object compacted of changes and hopes that forced his thoughts onward, and carried them far away from their old eager pacing towards the same blank limit—carried them away to new things that would come with the coming years, when Eppie would have learned to understand how her father Silas cared for her; and made him look for images of that time in the ties and charities that bound together the families of his neighbours. The gold had asked that he should sit weaving longer and longer, deafened and blinded more and more to all things except the monotony of his loom and the repetition of his web; but Eppie called him away from his weaving, and made him think all its pauses a holiday, reawakening his senses with her fresh life, even to the old winter-flies that came crawling forth in the early sunshine, and warming him into joy because *she* had joy. (184)

All the aspects of the tale that have impressed themselves most forcefully on the reader's imagination in the previous chapters are present here: the emphasis on shrinking and darkness, the equation of the gold and the child, the distinction between means and ends in terms of definitions of self and that which is beyond self, the imagery of weaving and the significance of the web that is woven, and the imagery of insects—here the water-flies, a little later the ladybirds—showing how "the little child had come to link him once more with the whole world." The passage ends with the repetition of the word "joy," which is what Eppie brings back into his life for the first time since his own childhood. "Joy" is the same thing as that combination of "hope" and "forward-looking thoughts" that appeared in the epigraph from Wordsworth, and "joy" too is a quintessentially Wordsworthian word. The child of the "Immortality Ode" is a "Child of Joy"; the poet's sister will remember him with "healing thoughts / Of tender joy" at the end of "Tintern Abbey";[2] and in "Michael" the old shepherd tells his son that "all thy life has been my daily joy" ("Michael," 345). The point about this distinctively Wordsworthian joy is that it is not an excitable or even very immediate sensation of happiness, but a steady and continuous feeling of well-being issuing from a person's sense of relationship with his own real past and expected future, and with that of his fellow beings. This is what Eppie achieves for Silas. By reawakening in him that "instinctive tenderness" ("Michael", 152) that managed to surface from time to time in the old days—when he performed an act of charity to Sally Oates, for example, or when he accepted the charity of the villagers in the Rainbow—she makes it possible for him to reestablish connections with the past that are expressed in language nearly identical to Wordsworth's: the "old quiverings of tenderness" (168) that reproduce those of the shepherd in the poem. George Eliot writes, "As the child's mind was growing into knowledge, his mind was growing into memory: as her life unfolded, his soul, long stupefied in a cold narrow prison, was unfolding too, and trembling gradually into full consciousness" (185). The process of "growing into memory" is better served by the past continuous tense of condensed description than by the past definite and historic present tenses of drama, dialogue, and scene. Although the tense changes, the method of condensed description continues in the second part of the novel, 16 years later, when we are still being told that "with reawakening sensibilities, memory also reawakened," and that Silas had "begun to ponder over the elements of his old faith, and blend them with his new impressions, till he recovered a consciousness of unity between his past and present" (202).

Epilogue: Part 2 of
Silas Marner

The harsh truth about Part 2 of Silas Marner is that it is superfluous as far as the history of Eppie and Silas is concerned, but absolutely necessary to complete the history of Godfrey Cass. The end of chapter 14 sounds like the end of the whole novel in so far as it is about Silas: "In old days there were angels who came and took men by the hand and led them away from the city of destruction. We see no white-winged angels now. But yet men are led away from threatening destruction: a hand is put into theirs, which leads them forth gently towards a calm and bright land, so that they look no more backward; and the hand may be a little child's" (190–91). Nothing could sound more final than that. The fable of the hoard of gold that turned into the golden-haired child is over. From Silas's point of view, there is no need for the gold to be discovered, and since our interest in Eppie is wholly dependent on our interest in him, there is no need for Eppie's future history to be recorded either. The things we are told about Silas and Eppie are the things we already knew. "At first," he says to her, "I'd a sort o'feeling came across me now and then . . . as if you might be changed into the gold again; for sometimes, turn my head which way I would, I seemed to see the gold; and I thought I should be glad if I could feel it, and find it was come back. But that didn't last long. After a bit, I should have thought it was a curse come again, if it had drove you from me, for I'd got to feel the need o' your looks and your voice and the touch o' your little fingers" (226).

The interview between Silas and Eppie and Godfrey and Nancy simply confirms, from the Marner side of the story, our sense of the reciprocal bond between father and adopted daughter. The condensed account of their life together provided in chapter 14 makes it unthinkable that it should be other than reciprocal. Any other outcome would have had to occupy much more space than the three or four chapters given over to it in the novel.

For Godfrey and Nancy it is different. Here there is much more that we want to know. It is right, then, that the paragraph just quoted from the end of chapter 14 should not be the last chapter of Part 1, but should be followed by a short chapter about Godfrey's engagement to Nancy, his looking forward to having children of his own whom he can acknowledge and care for, and his recognition of the father's duty he must accept with regard to Eppie. With Godfrey as the center of attention, there is a great deal that can happen and that can engage the reader's attention and, possibly, sympathy. The trouble is that it is likely to involve Eppie, and if it involves Eppie it is bound to involve Silas, too. In Part 1, the knitting together of the fortunes of the cottage and the Red House is the main source of the strength of the novel. But that is because it is either invisible or unacknowledged by the characters who live in those places. Now, whatever happens is likely to happen as a result of one or both of two things taking place: the discovery of Dunstan's remains and the disclosure of Eppie's identity. The one need not bring the other in its train, but it is likely to do so, and in the even it does. It does, not because of any logical connection between the two facts, but because the exposure of Dunsey's skeleton, as a result of Godfrey's own actions in arranging for the Stone-pit to be drained, brings so vividly before his mind the idea that "everything comes to light . . . sooner or later" (223). If this, why not his fathering of Eppie? And remember, his own whip—with his own name engraved on the handle—is the principal means of identification of the corpse.

It is a hidden part of himself, the rejected self of 16 years seclusion that was the indirect cause of Dunsey's drowning, that is uncovered along with Dunsey's remains in the pit. The suggestive horror of the event far outweighs in his mind its actually fairly small implications for his future with Nancy. In fact the logical gap, or causal vacuum, between the discovery of the skeleton and the confession to Nancy reveals a great deal about Godfrey's inner life during his 16 years of marriage. These have been 16 years of childlessness that Godfrey has obscurely understood to have been caused by his rejection of that other child whose identity, he feels, must now be brought to light.

Godfrey cast only a single glance at the face of his dead first wife when he went with Dolly and Mr. Kimble to the cottage on the night of the New Year's dance. But he remembers her last look so well "that at the end of sixteen years every line in the worn face was present to him when he told the full story of this night" (175). We were told this back in chapter 13. That is to say, we were alerted to Godfrey's buried remorse long before it was disinterred along with his brother's corpse. The dramatic event that forces him to tell the full story is therefore of great interest to us. Indeed, it is of such great interest that George Eliot doesn't have to dwell on it. It happens offstage, sandwiched between a casual reference to the draining of the pit and the lengthy confrontation between Godfrey and Nancy that follows. Godfrey's announcement of what has happened has the directness and simplicity of a ballad: " 'The Stone-pit has gone dry suddenly—from the draining, I suppose: and there he lies—has lain for sixteen years, wedged between two great stones. There's his watch and seals and there's my gold-handled hunting-whip, with my name on: he took it away, without my knowing, the day he went hunting on Wildfire, the last time he was seen' " (222).

Nothing more needs to be said, apart from the conclusion, equally bluntly spoken by Godfrey, that "Dunstan was the man that robbed Silas Marner" (222). George Eliot reminds us that Nancy had been "bred up to regard even a distant kinship with crime as a dishonour" (223), and we feel the full force of that fact all the more emphatically as a result of the characterization of Nancy that has preceded this

scene in chapter 17. There, the impression we received of her at the
Red House all those years ago is subtly and painfully reinforced. She
betrays the same "mingled pride and ignorance of the world's evil"
(219) as she did then, equally moderated by "the spirit of rectitude
and the sense of responsibility for the effect of her conduct on others"
that was present before her marriage and before the loss of her first
child. It is perfectly understandable that Godfrey is shocked by what
he has found out about Dunsey and the money, because he knows
how difficult it will be for Nancy to come to terms with the taintedness
she must feel at being associated with the crime. The existence of
Godfrey's child must come as an even greater and less welcome surprise
to her. She had attributed her childlessness to an act of Providence.
She had accepted that to have children was something that for her
"was not meant to be" (217). Ironically it was this way of looking at
things, bred in her out of her attachment to principles based on a very
unsatisfactory but deeply excavated theological foundation, which persuaded her not to agree to Godfrey's earlier proposal that they should
adopt Eppie as their own child. "How could she," then, "have any
mercy for faults that must seem so black to her, with her simple, severe
notions?" (224). No wonder "Godfrey felt all the bitterness of an error
that was not simply futile, but had defeated its own end."

By the time we arrive with Godfrey and Nancy at the cottage we
understand very well what a fraught interview will follow. Opportuni-
ties for the display of divided loyalties, embarrassed self-regard and
self-justification, conflicting moral judgments, and compromised authority are legion. There is a great deal George Eliot can do with
Godfrey and Nancy in this scene. But there is next to nothing she can
do with Silas and Eppie. Theirs is obviously going to be a united front
of loving parent and dutiful child. And this in turn means that the
reader's attention is likely to be very unevenly distributed between the
two parties, throughout the confrontation.

And so it proves. Silas's and Eppie's behavior is as expected.
Everything they do is exemplary of their very simple characters. Silas's
complex attitude toward his reputation, his gold, his religion, and his
standing in the community has been simplified with the coming of

Eppie, and Eppie is the symbol of his salvation. The fairy tale has ended with the exchange of the gold for the child. In naturalistic terms, the return of the gold could only perplex and complicate the relationship between Silas and Eppie and the village. It is not allowed to do so because the ending of the Silas/Eppie story is simply a long drawn-out way of saying that they lived happily ever after. But Godfrey and Nancy are quite another matter. For each of them the coming to light of what happened 16 years ago is a real test of character that is subtly imperfect. Godfrey's sense of shame and guilt is awkwardly compromised by the "exalted consciousness" (235) of doing the right thing with which he sets out for Silas's cottage. He was "possessed with all-important feelings" about what is due to him, as well as what is due from him to those he has sinned against. In this respect Nancy's sense of what is and is not right doesn't help him to follow a proper course of action. Like him, she fails to understand the claims of filial piety that belong to the adoptive father:

> Even Nancy, with all the acute sensibility of her own affections, shared her husband's view, that Marner was not justifiable in his wish to retain Eppie, after her real father had avowed himself. She felt that it was a very hard trial for the poor weaver, but her code allowed no question that a father by blood must have a claim above that of any foster-father. Besides Nancy, used all her life to plenteous circumstances and the privileges of "respectability," could not enter into the pleasures which early nurture and habit connect with all the little aims and efforts of the poor who are born poor: to her mind, Eppie, in being restored to her birthright, was entering on a too long withheld but unquestionable good. (232–33)

It is exactly the same with Godfrey, who "was not prepared to enter with lively appreciation into other people's feelings counteracting his virtuous resolves" (230). In both cases a narrowness of feeling, an inability to press beyond the limitations imposed on their way of looking at the world by their upbringing and their restricted range of experiences, makes it impossible for them to understand the quality of Silas's love for Eppie and therefore to acknowledge the right to her

that this love confers upon him. Instead, they interpret Eppie's decision
to remain with her foster father and to marry Aaron as a judgment
on themselves. Silas has already pointed out, without malice, that
"repentance doesn't alter what's been going on for sixteen years"
(231), and Godfrey transforms this statement of fact into an accusation
against him. When he says that "there's debts we can't pay like money
debts, by paying extra for the years that have slipped by" (236), he is
merely repeating what Silas has said. But he goes further when he
interprets his loss of Eppie as an act of destiny, weighing guilt and
punishment in an equal scale: "I wanted to pass for childless once,
Nancy—I shall pass for childless now against my wish" (231). To his
claim that "it's part of my punishment," Nancy can reply only in
accordance with a "spirit of rectitude" that "would not let her try to
soften this edge of what she felt to be a just compunction" (237).

Godfrey is severe on himself, and Nancy is severe on Godfrey,
but no more so than George Eliot. She, too, felt that there was an
almost divine logic in the doctrine of consequences, an "orderly sequence by which the seed brings forth a crop after its kind" (127). She
had found deep down in Godfrey's consciousness, "half-smothered by
passionate desire and dread," a sense that "he ought to accept the
consequences of his deeds" (174), and this was *before* he even saw
Molly's dead face on the pillow. This doctrine of consequences is
what remained of her own religious experience in her evangelical and
Methodist youth. It has something in common with the dour and
unpitying doctrine of the Calvinists at Lantern Yard. In the novels the
"orderly sequence" is capable of manifesting itself in the remorseless
logic of Godfrey's collapse into compromise with his own best principles and the mediocrity of spirit that follows. Or it shows itself in the
chapter of accidents that results in Silas Marner's initially "impressible
self-doubting nature" (57) being further undermined and then recon-
structed on the basis of a more secure understanding of what that
nature really is.

In other works George Eliot calls this orderly sequence "Neme-
sis": "Consequences are unpitying. Our deeds carry their terrible consequences . . .—consequences that are hardly ever confined to

ourselves.''[1] So it is for Godfrey. Although he cannot understand why Eppie wishes to remain with Silas rather than go back to the Red House with him and Nancy, his renunciation of her in the light of Silas's higher claim is very proper and utterly in keeping with George Eliot's stern view of the remedial power of renunciation. According to her, there is a kind of heroism in renunciation that is the secular equivalent of the sufferings of the martyrs. In a review article for the *Westminster* six years earlier, she had written about the beauty and heroism of renunciation. This is the unsentimental moralist in George Eliot speaking, but in the secular-mystical tones of her beloved Goethe, especially in acts 4 and 5 of the second part of *Faust*. She differs from Lantern Yard in her view that although consequences are unpitying, we should not be. Indeed the remorseless juggernaut of cause and consequence forces on us a duty of sympathy with those—all our fellow human beings—who experience its terrible progress over their lives. Let us, she writes in *Adam Bede*, ''love that . . . beauty . . . which lies . . . in the secret of deep human sympathy'' (*Bede*, 224). Even, presumably, when it is called forth by people like Godfrey and Nancy who are incapable of feeling it themselves, who ''had not had . . . the power, of entering intimately into all that was exceptional in the weaver's experience'' (218).

This is another Wordsworthian idea, akin to the ''tranquil sympathies'' that ''steal upon the meditative mind, / And grow with thought'' in the first book of *The Excursion*.[2] Godfrey is right to consider himself justly punished. Nancy's spirit of rectitude rightly makes it impossible for her to pretend things are otherwise than they are. Nevertheless, her power of sympathy, at this crisis in their relationship, is as relevant to the circumstances as is her sense of justice. She, too, advises resignation in the face of adversity, and she includes herself in this advice, since she will not take advantage of her knowledge of Godfrey's past misdeeds to reject him now that the truth has come to light.

There is a connection between this perception of the remorselessness of consequences and the attendant duty of human sympathy, and the kind of writing George Eliot recommends in her essays and produces in her own novels. What we have discovered in *Silas Marner* is the alternation of fable or romance (which she does not recommend), and documentary realism or novel (which she does). In *Silas Marner* neither supplants the other. In some places the element of fable or fairy tale is more pronounced, in other places the element of prosaic verisimilitude. But the strategy is dictated by George Eliot's intentions, which are basically of the second, prosaic kind. She uses the fairy-tale material not so much to suggest the irreducible and therefore inexpressible mysteries of the human condition, as to sketch out a preliminary scenario that is later to be rendered both morally and psychologically plausible through a process of realistic blurring, softening, and substitution.

There are two kinds of fairy-tale writing here. One is the dramatic, even melodramatic, handling of fantasy material (the theft of the gold by Dunstan, the appearance of the child on the hearth of Silas's cottage). The other is the almost imperceptible and continuous hum and murmur of a subterranean fabular theme (the allusions to the story of King Midas or of *The Winter's Tale*) beneath the surface outlines of a mainly realistic story. The fact is, though, that these outlines are not merely superficial. They help us to penetrate to the core of the novel's thematic content—the dense network of psychological conditions and moral judgments and invitation to sympathetic understanding that constitute the bulk of all George Eliot's writing. True, the detail of that network is more evident in the Godfrey/Nancy part of the story and rather less so in the Silas Marner part. This is unusual for George Eliot. Normally all of her principal characters are explained as thoroughly as Godfrey and Nancy. But we have seen that within the fairy-tale ambience of the Silas Marner story there is a good deal of local psychological drama. There is also some naturalistic description (after Silas's entry at the Rainbow) and character analysis (in the comparison between Silas and William Dane in chapter 1). This does a great deal to make Silas's character and predicament credible, even if it lacks something of the incomprehensible mystery that adds a surprising depth to some of the characters of, say, American romance.

George Eliot is most explicit about her intentions in an early chapter (chapter 3) of *The Mill on the Floss*. Here Mr. Tulliver has asked his friend Mr. Riley, the auctioneer, to give him an opinion about a teacher for his son Tom. Mr. Riley suggests that Mr. Stelling is the man, but Tulliver is unsure about Riley's motives. Without good reason, though. George Eliot explains:

> And he had really given himself the trouble of recommending Mr. Stelling to his friend Tulliver without any positive expectation of a solid, definite advantage resulting to himself, notwithstanding the subtle indications to the contrary which might have misled a too sagacious observer. For there is nothing more widely misleading than sagacity if it happens to get on a wrong scent; and sagacity persuaded that men usually act and speak from distinct motives, with a consciously proposed end in view, is certain to waste its energies on imaginary game. Plotting covetousness and deliberate contrivance, in order to compass a selfish end, are nowhere abundant but in the world of the dramatist. They demand too intense a mental action for many of our fellow-parishioners to be guilty of them. It is easy enough to spoil the lives of our neighbours without taking so much trouble: we can do it by lazy acquiescence and lazy omission, by trivial falsities for which we hardly know a reason, by small frauds neutralized by small extravagancies, by maladroit flatteries, and clumsily improvised insinuation. We live from hand to mouth, most of us, with a small family of immediate desires; we do little else than snatch a morsel to satisfy the hungry brood, rarely thinking of seed-corn or the next year's crop.[3]

In *Silas Marner*, as in *The Mill in the Floss*, George Eliot is enough of a Victorian novelist to be unable to construct her story without a great deal more melodramatic contrivance than she suggests is necessary here. But she is more honest in her use of it. The fabular elements do not pretend to be anything else, on the whole, and therefore convince on their own terms more than the fabular elements in her more soberly realistic narratives do. Even so, much that is best in *Silas Marner* has more to do with lazy omissions and trivial falsities than with plotting covetousness and deliberate contrivance. Even Dunstan's theft of the gold has more in it of self-deception and wishful thinking than it has of deeply meditated intrigue or conspiracy. And Godfrey's misfortunes arise entirely out of "small frauds neutralised [or not] by small extravagancies." Probably the most melodramatic character in the novel is William Dane. He disappears after the first chapter, and even there his lies about Silas are explained by the corruption of his Calvinist faith and his envy of Silas's engagement to Sarah.

The fairy-tale outlines of the melodramatic plot have to be softened and obscured so as to bring into focus the basically explicable motives and attitudes of the characters. In *Middlemarch*, Dorothea's perception of the passionate egotism of her husband, Casaubon, becomes so sharp as to banish all thoughts not only of melodrama but of tragedy. Everything about him except his egotism was "below the level of tragedy" (*Middlemarch*, 460). Awareness of tragedy involves not just pity, but, Aristotle wrote, terror also. We need to be as much aware of the general condition, in which we ourselves are included, as of the particular instance, which stands free of any merely selfish regard. George Eliot's is an art of the particular instance: of Silas, Godfrey, and Nancy, rather than the miser, the rake, and the saintly young girl. Therefore her art is depressed "below the level of tragedy" in the higher interest of pure compassion. Compassion transcends justice—which must also be done, and, where possible, be seen to be done. Compassion is more inward, more secretive, felt even when it is not seen. In her compassion for Casaubon, Dorothea "was travelling into the remoteness of pure pity" (*Middlemarch*, 402). It is what George Eliot want us to feel for Silas, and later for Godfrey. It is what Nancy can almost bring herself to feel for Godfrey. In the end it is what Godfrey is brought to feel for himself, along with at least a residue of the justice Nancy and his own conscience have persuaded him is not to be ignored: "Well, perhaps it isn't too late to mend a bit there. Though it *is* too late to mend some things, say what they will" (237).

Notes and References

Chapter 1

1. Richard Chase, *The American Novel and Its Tradition* (London: G. Bell and Sons, 1958); hereafter cited as Chase.

Chapter 2

1. Henry James, review of *Life* by John Cross, *Atlantic Monthly* (May 1885), reprinted in David Carroll, ed., *George Eliot: The Critical Heritage* (London: Routledge & Kegan Paul, 1971), 502; hereafter cited as Carroll.

Chapter 3

1. Anonymous, review of *Silas Marner*, *Dublin University Magazine* (April 1862), reprinted in Carroll, 192; hereafter cited as Carroll.

2. Anonymous, review of *Silas Marner*, *Saturday Review* (April 1861), reprinted in Carroll, 170–76; hereafter cited as Carroll.

3. Leslie Stephen, obituary article, *Cornhill Magazine* (February 1881), reprinted in Carroll, 464–86; hereafter cited as Carroll.

4. Richard Simpson, "George Eliot's Novels," *Home and Foreign Review* (October 1863), reprinted in Carroll, 221–50; hereafter cited as Carroll.

5. Virginia Woolf, in *Times Literary Supplement* (20 November 1919); reprinted in *The Common Reader* (London: Hogarth, 1948), 205–18.

6. F.R. Leavis, "George Eliot. The Early Phase," in *The Great Tradition* (London: Chatto and Windus, 1948), 28–47; hereafter cited as Leavis, 1948.

7. Queenie Leavis, ed., *Silas Marner* (Harmondsworth: Penguin, 1967); hereafter cited as Leavis, 1967.

8. George Sturt, *Change in the Village* (1912; London: Caliban Books, 1984); hereafter cited as Sturt. Sturt (1863–1927) wrote under the pseudonym of "George Bourne." As well as *Change in the Village*, he was the author of many books about nineteenth-century English village life, including *The Wheelwright's Shop*, published under his own name in 1923.

9. John Holloway, "Introduction" to *Silas Marner* (London: J.M. Dent & Sons, Everyman ed., 1975); hereafter cited as Holloway.

10. David Carroll, "Revising the Oracles of Religion," in *The Mill on the Floss and Silas Marner*, Casebook Series, ed. R. P. Draper (London: Macmillan, 1977), 188–216.

Chapter 4

1. William Wordsworth, "Michael," in W.M. Merchant, ed., *Wordsworth, Poetry and Prose* (London: Rupert Hart-Davis, 1969), 193–205; hereafter cited as "Michael."

2. William Wordsworth, "The Thorn," in Merchant, 128–35.

3. William Wordsworth, "The Mad Mother," in Merchant, 80–88.

4. William Wordsworth, "Anecdote for Fathers," in Merchant, 57–60.

5. George Eliot, "Letter," reprinted in *The Mill on the Floss and Silas Marner*, Casebook Series, ed. R. P. Draper (London: Macmillan, 1977), 38; hereafter cited as Draper.

Chapter 5

1. *The George Eliot Letters*, ed. G. S. Haight (New Haven: Yale University Press, 1954–78), vol. 3, 382; hereafter cited as *Letters*.

2. John Bunyan, *The Pilgrim's Progress* (Harmondsworth: Penguin,) hereafter cited as Bunyan. *The Pilgrim's Progress* was among the most popular books in Victorian households of all classes. There was a copy in George Eliot's father's house which she must have read before her eighth birthday. "There were then few books for children, in the Evans household, at least, but she had *The Pilgrim's Progress*, *The Vicar of Wakefield*, *Aesop's Fables* with pictures" (*Letters*, 7).

3. Donald Davie, *A Gathered Church: The Literature of the English Dissenting Interest 1700–1930*, Clark Lectures 1976 (London: Routledge & Kegan Paul, 1978; New York: Oxford University Press, 1978). See especially Lecture 4, "Dissent and the Evangelicals, 1800–1850."

4. John Bunyan, "A Confession of my Faith." See R.L. Greaves, *John Bunyan, Courtenay Studies in Reformation Theology* (Appleford England, 1969), chapters 1, 2, and 6.

5. "Janet's Repentance," in *Scenes from Clerical Life* (Oxford: Clarendon edition, 1985), 253; hereafter cited as *Scenes*.

6. G.M. Trevelyan, *English Social History* (London: Longmans, 1944), 470.

Chapter 6

1. Asa Briggs, *The Age of Improvement* (London: Longmans, 1959), 59.

2. George Crabbe, *The Borough*, in Howard Mills, ed., *George Crabbe, Tales. 1812* (Cambridge: Cambridge University Press, 1967), 95–106.

3. Henry James, "The Novels of George Eliot," *Atlantic Monthly* (1866), reprinted in George Eliot, *The Mill on the Floss and Silas Marner*, Casebook Series, ed. R. P. Draper (London: Macmillan, 1977), 67.

4. George Eliot, "The Natural History of German Life," *Westminster Review* 64 (July 1856), reprinted in *The Essays of George Eliot*, ed. Thomas Pinney (London: Routledge & Kegan Paul, 1963), 266–99; hereafter cited as "German Life."

5. See Hugh Witemayer, *George Eliot and the Visual Arts* (New Haven and London: Yale University Press, 1979), 139–40.

6. Joseph Langhorne, "The Country Justice," in Donald Davie, ed., *The Late Augustans* (London: Heinemann, 1958), 71–92.

7. For George Eliot on Wilkie see *Letters* (vol. 1), 71: "Mine is too often a world such as Wilkie can so well paint, a *walled-in* world, furnished with all the details which he remembers so accurately"; and "German Life," 270, where she praises Scott's reference to Wilkie's cottage-pictures in his novel *The Antiquary*.

Chapter 7

1. In Roger Lonsdale, ed., *The New Oxford Book of Eighteenth Century Verse* (Oxford: Oxford University Press, 1984), 617–20.

2. The history of the free indirect style, or *style indirect libre*, is traced in Stephen Ullmann, *Style in the French Novel* (Cambridge: Cambridge University Press, 1957).

Chapter 8

1. *Middlemarch* (Harmondsworth: Penguin, 1965), 890; hereafter cited as *Middlemarch*.

2. William Wordsworth, "Tintern Abbey," in Merchant, 152–56.

Chapter 9

1. *Adam Bede* (Harmondsworth: Penguin, 1980), 217; hereafter cited as *Bede*.

2. William Wordsworth, *The Excursion*, in Merchant, 663–94.

3. *The Mill on the Floss* (Harmondsworth: Penguin, 1979), 74–75.

Bibliography

Primary Sources

The new Oxford Clarendon edition of the Works of George Eliot is in process of replacing the older Standard Editions of 1869 ("Cabinet") and 1897. So far, four of the novels have been published: *The Mill on the Floss*. Edited by G. S. Haight. 1980; *Felix Holt, the Radical*. Edited by F. C. Thomson. 1980; *Daniel Deronda*. Edited by B. Handley. 1984; and *Scenes of Clerical Life*. Edited by T. A. Noble. 1985. There are easily accessible editions of all of the novels in both Penguin and Everyman paperbacks. As mentioned earlier, the editions of *Silas Marner* under both of these imprints (Harmondsworth: Penguin, 1967, edited by Q. D. Leavis; London: Everyman, 1977, edited by John Holloway) contain excellent introductions. See also the Rinehart edition, with introduction by Jerome Thale, 1962.

The Essays of George Eliot. Edited by Thomas Pinney. London: Routledge & Kegan Paul, 1963.

The George Eliot Letters. 9 vols. Edited by G. S. Haight. New Haven and London: Yale University Press, 1954–78.

Secondary Sources

Biographies

Haight, Gordon S. *George Eliot, A Biography*. Oxford and New York: Oxford University Press, 1968. Still very much the best biography of George Eliot. Sober, very detailed, and utterly reliable.

Redinger, Ruby. *George Eliot: The Emergent Self*. New York: Alfred A. Knopf, 1975.

Taylor, Ina. *George Eliot: Woman of Contradictions*. London: Weidenfeld, 1989.

Critical Studies

Beer, Gillian. *George Eliot*. Key Women Writers Series. Brighton, England: Harvester, 1986.

Bennett, Joan. *George Eliot, Her Mind and Art*. Cambridge: Cambridge University Press, 1948.

Bullet, Gerald. *George Eliot: Her Life and Books*. London: Collins, 1947.

Carpenter, Mary Wilson. *George Eliot and the Landscape of Time: Narrative Form and Protestant Apocalyptic History*. Chapel Hill: University of North Carolina Press, 1986.

Hardy, Barbara. *The Novels of George Eliot*. Oxford and New York: Oxford University Press, 1959.

Harvey, W. J. *The Art of George Eliot*. London: Chatto and Windus, 1963.

Jones, R. T. *George Eliot*. Cambridge: Cambridge University Press, 1970.

Knoepflmacher, U. C. *George Eliot's Early Novels: The Limits of Realism*. Berkeley and Los Angeles: University of California Press, 1968.

Thale, Jerome. *The Novels of George Eliot*. London and New York: Columbia University Press, 1959.

Witemayer, Hugh. *George Eliot and the Visual Arts*. London and New Haven: Yale University Press, 1979.

Articles in Journals and Parts of Books

Allott, Miriam. "George Eliot in the 1860's." *Victorian Studies* 5 (1961–62): 93–108. Really spans from 1863 (*Romola*) to 1868 (*The Spanish Gypsy*), i.e., an inquiry into what went wrong after *Silas Marner*. But the descriptions of negative qualities of the novels of the later 1860s help to bring into focus the positive qualities of what preceded them.

Carroll, D. R. "An Image of Disenchantment in the Novels of George Eliot." *Review of English Studies* 11 n.s. (1960): 29–41. No references to *Silas Marner*, but the image of the ruin is applicable to George Eliot's representation of the characters of both Silas and Godfrey Cass.

———. "*Silas Marner*: Reversing the Oracles of Religion." *Literary Monographs*, no.1. 165–200. Madison, Milwaukee, and London: University of Wisconsin Press, 1967. Excellent appreciation of the influence of Feuerbach on the themes and structure of *Silas Marner*. See chapter 3 of the present study for further comment. Most of the essay is reproduced in Draper (listed under "Collections").

Dessner, L. J. "The Autobiographical Matrix of *Silas Marner*." *Studies in the Novel* 2 (1979): 251–82. Compare with Hawes (below) on the relationship between the book and the life. This is a longer essay, which refers to George Eliot's letters written before and during composition of *Silas Marner* to show how depressive emotional states are put to successful use in fiction.

Hawes, Donald. "Chance in *Silas Marner*." *English* 31 (1982): 213–18. Argues that blemishes in George Eliot's discursive prose, notably the moralizing passage on "favourable Chance" at the end of chapter 9, might have been avoided if she had given way to her inclination to produce a metrical version of the story. A dotty proposition, surprisingly well argued.

Holloway, John. "George Eliot." In *The Victorian Sage*, 111–57. London: Macmillan, 1953. Examines how George Eliot expresses a general vision of life through the organization of detail in her novels. Three pages devoted to *Silas Marner*, plus other occasional references.

House, Humphrey. "Qualities of George Eliot's Unbelief." In *All in Due Time*, 109–15. London: Hart Davis, 1955. Good incidental comments on the "theology" of *Silas Marner* from an excellent critic.

Leavis, F. R. "George Eliot: The Early Phase." In *The Great Tradition*, 28–47. London: Chatto & Windus, 1948.

Lerner, Laurence. *The Truthtellers*. 28–66, 235–78. London: Chatto & Windus, 1967. Sympathetically corrects Leavis's judgement of George Eliot's idealism. Mainly on *Middlemarch*, but with some application to the shorter fiction.

Masters, Donald C. "George Eliot and the Evangelicals." *Dalhousie Review* 41 (1962): 505–12.

McLaverty, James. "Comtean Fetishism in *Silas Marner*." *Nineteenth Century Fiction* 36 (1982): 318–36. Complements Carroll (cited here) on Feuerbach by emphasizing the importance of the ideas of Auguste Comte in *Silas Marner*. Refers especially to two of Comte's later works, *The Catechism of Positive Religion* (1852) and *System of Positive Polity* (1854), which explain the idea of "fetishism" as a link between the first and last stages in Comte's religion of humanity.

Milner, Ian. "Structure and Quality in *Silas Marner*." *Studies in English Literature, 1500–1900* 6 (1966): 717–29. A good essay on *Silas Marner* as a moral fable that successfully dramatizes the experience of alienation.

Parsons, Coleman O. "Background Material Illustrative of *Silas Marner*." *Notes and Queries* 191 (1946): 266–70. A useful study of *Silas Marner* in the tradition of stories about misers and misanthropes. These include novels by Balzac, Scott, Dickens, Emily Appleton, and Cyrus Redding.

Also Wordsworth's *Excursion*. But the principal comparison is with John Wilson's *The Foresters* and *The Trials of Margaret Lyndsay*. Wilson was a contemporary, and was often referred to as a disciple, of Wordsworth.

―――. "The Authority of the Past in George Eliot's Novels." *Nineteenth Century Fiction* 21 (1966): 131–47. Not much on *Silas Marner*, but comments on George Eliot's "emotional naturalism" and on her espousal of Wordsworthian notions of natural piety can be applied fruitfully to this novel, as well as to others dealt with here at greater length.

Pinney, Thomas. "George Eliot's Reading of Wordsworth: The Record." *Victorian Newsletter* 24 (Fall 1963): 20–22. A bare, factual account of the evidence of George Eliot's reading of Wordsworth, including the references in *Silas Marner*. Doesn't attempt a critical application.

Simpson, Peter. "Crisis and Recovery: William Wordsworth, George Eliot, and *Silas Marner*." *University of Toronto Quarterly* 48 (1979): 95–114. The first part of this essay, documenting the influence of Wordsworth on George Eliot, is helpful. The second part, on her symbolic self-identification with Silas Marner for purposes of vicarious self-integration, is less convincing, but not as silly as this rather condensed description might suggest.

Swann, Brian. "*Silas Marner* and the New Mythus." *Criticism* 18 (Spring 1976): 101–21. The imagery of *Silas Marner* is an effective part of George Eliot's practice of combining realism and fairy tale in a narrative of moral and spiritual regeneration.

Thale, Jerome. "George Eliot's Fable for her Time." *College English* 19 (1958): 141–46. A very good essay about *Silas Marner* in the tradition of nineteenth-century crisis and conversion literature. The two stories, of Silas and Godfrey Cass, are different expressions of the same theme. The contrast between their outcomes (happy and unhappy) and between their narrative methods (pastoral and realistic) accounts for George Eliot's unusual success in resolving her artistic difficulties.

Thomson, Fred C. "The Theme of Alienation in *Silas Marner*." *Nineteenth Century Fiction* 20 (1965): 69–84. Argues that *Silas Marner* is George Eliot's first and only partially successful attempt to convey her idea of tragic destiny through the agencies of the alienated character and the double plot. But any piece of work that places such a high valuation on *Felix Holt* must fail to convince.

Collections Especially Relevant to *Silas Marner*

Carroll, David, ed. "*Silas Marner*." In *George Eliot: The Critical Heritage* 168–95. London: Routledge & Kegan Paul, 1971.

Selected Bibliography

Draper, R. P., ed. *George Eliot, The Mill on the Floss and Silas Marner.* Casebook Series. London: Macmillan, 1977.

Bibliographies

Fulmer, Constance Marie. *George Eliot: A Reference Guide.* Boston: G. K. Hall & Co., 1977.

Higdon, D. L. "A Bibliography of George Eliot Criticism 1971–1977." *Bulletin of Bibliography* 37 (no.2, Spring–June): 1980.

Knoepflmacher, U. C. "George Eliot." In *Victorian Fiction: A Second Guide to Research*, edited by G. Ford. New York: Modern Languages Association of America, 1978.

Levine, G. L. (with assistance of Patrica O'Hare). *An Annotated Critical Bibliography of George Eliot.* Brighton, England: Harvester Press, 1988.

Marshall, William H. "A Selective Bibliography of Writings about George Eliot, to 1965." *Bulletin of Bibliography* 25 (nos. 3–4): 1967.

Index

Arbury Hall, 10, 47
Arminianism, 41
Atlantic Monthly, 14
Austen, Jane: *Emma*, 48

Balaam, 40
Balzac, Honoré de: *Eugenie Grandet*, 92
Baptists, General and Particular, 33–34, 41
Bennett, Joan: *George Eliot, Her Mind and Her Art*, 17
Blackwood, John, 12, 103
Blanc, Jean Joseph Louis, 4
Breuer, Joseph, 39
Brontë, Charlotte, 78
Brontë, Emily: *Wuthering Heights*, 7, 78
Brouwer, Adrien, 52
Bullett, Gerald: *George Eliot: Her Life and Books*, 17
Bunyan, John: *Pilgrim's Progress, The*, 7, 8, 30–31, 36, 38, 40, 74, 97
Burton, Sir Frederic, 10–11

Calvinism, 35–38, 40
Carroll, David: "Revising the Oracles of Religion," 20
Carus, Victor, 5
catalepsy, 39

Chapman, John, 4, 28
characters in *Silas Marner*
Bryce, Mr., 59, 79
Cass, Dunstan, 9, 28, 62, 68–70, 71, 79–80, 84–87
Cass, Godfrey, 9, 24, 25, 56, 58, 62, 66, 67, 68–75, 77, 81, 85, 88, 107–15
Cass, Squire, 64, 65–67
Cox, Mr., 80
Crackenthorp, Mr., 41, 76, 82
Dane, William, 38, 40, 41–42, 47, 115
Dowlas, Mr., 56–57
Drumlow, Mr., 56–57
Eppie, 25, 32, 39, 48, 71, 99–105, 106
Farren, Molly, 9, 24, 50, 74, 77, 111
Gunn, the Misses, 76–77, 78, 80
Jay, Betty, 80–81
Kimble, Mr., 108
Ladbrook, Miss, 76–80
Lammeter, Mr., 67
Lammeter, Nancy, 24, 25, 56, 62, 63, 71, 74, 75–79, 81, 88, 107–10
Lammeter, Priscilla, 77, 78
Lundy, Mr., 55, 56
Macey Solomon, 29, 38, 56–57, 59, 60, 64

characters in *Silis Marner* [*cont.*]
  Marner, Silas, 9, 19, 23–24,
    25–26, 28–44, 45, 48, 49, 50,
    63, 86, 87, 88–105, 106–15
  Oates, Sally, 29, 105
  Osgood, Miss, 56
  Osgood, Mr., 64
  Osgood, Mrs., 81, 92
  Rodney, Jem, 28, 40, 50, 98
  Sarah, 115
  Snell, Mr., 55–57
  "Snuff" (the spaniel) and Speed
    (the deerhound), 75
  Tookey, Mr., 55–56, 59
  "Wildfire" (the horse), 58, 70,
    72, 79, 81
  Winthrop, Aaron, 111
  Winthrop, Dollie, 32, 33, 47, 48,
    59–61, 99, 108
Chase, Richard: *American Novel
  and its Tradition, The*, 7–8, 82
Congregationalism, 35
Cornhill Magazine, 5
Crabbe, George, 51; *Borough, The*,
  50; *Parish Register, The*, 50
Cross, John Walter: *Life of George
  Eliot*, 10

Dallas, E. S., 14
Darwin, Charles, 4
Davie, Donald: *Gathered Church,
  A*, 37
Defoe, Daniel: *Journal of the Plague
  Year, A*, 95; *Robinson Crusoe*,
  7
Dickens, Charles, 3, 12, 17, 54;
  Oliver Twist, 6, 78, 99
Draper, R. P., "Casebook" on *Silas
  Marner and Mill on the Floss,
  The*, 20
Dublin University (magazine), 13

Economist, 14
Eliot, George

WORKS
  Adam Bede, 6, 12, 13, 24, 37,
    76, 78, 112
  "Amos Barton," 47
  "Brother Jacob," 6
  Daniel Deronda, 45, 91
  Felix Holt, the Radical, 124
  "Janet's Repentance," 6, 37,
    41–44
  Middlemarch, 7, 10, 76, 90–91,
    115
  Mill on the Floss, The, 6, 10, 12,
    13, 16, 113–14
  Romola, 6, 12, 15
  Scenes of Clerical Life, 6, 12, 13,
    37, 41–44, 147
Evangelicalism, 42–43

Feuerbach, Ludwig Andreas:
  Essence of Christianity, The, 4,
    15, 44, 58
Fielding, Henry, 3, 6
Freud, Sigmund, 39
Froude, J. A., 4

Galt, John, 51
Gaskell, [Mrs] Elizabeth, 78
Gaskell, Peter, *Artists and
  Machinery*, 19
Goethe, Johann Wolfgang von, 4;
  Faust, 112
Gospels, The, 33

Hardy, Thomas: *Tess of the
  d'Urbervilles*, 49
Hawthorne, Nathaniel, 8;
  Tanglewood Tales, 101
Hennell, Charles, 34
Hennell, Sara, 36
Hephzibah, 33
Hogg, James: *Private Memoirs of a
  Justified Sinner, The*, 7
Holloway, John, 18, 19–20, 35

Index

Holmes, Oliver Wendell: *Elsie Venner*, 13
Home and Foreign Review, 14, 15–17
Hunt, William Holman, 51
Hutton, R. H., 14
Huxley, T. H., 4

Isaiah, Book of, 33

Jairus's daughter, 40
James, Henry, 10, 14, 15, 51, 52
Jonson, Ben: *Volpone*, 92

Langhorne, Joseph, "Country Justice, The," 52
Lardner, Ring, 54
Laurence, Samuel, 10
Lazarus, 40
Leavis, F. R.: *Great Tradition, The*, 17–18
Leavis, Q. D., 18–19, 36, 78
Lewes, George Henry, 5, 15
Lewis, Maria, 78
Liszt, Franz, 4

Mant's Bible, 5
Melville, Herman, 8; *Moby Dick*, 7
Midas, King of Phrygia, 101
Mill, John Stuart, 4
Molière: *L'Avare*, 92
Mommsen, Theodor, 4
Murillo, Bartolomé, Esteban, 51–52

New Republic, 4
Numbers, Book of, 40

Peacock, Thomas Love, 3
Poor Law, 50–51

"Red Rovier, The," 5
Reform Bill of 1832, 45–46
Rousseau, Jean Jacques, 4

Rumpelstiltskin, 102
Runyon, Damon, 54

Samuel, First Book of, 35
Saturday Review, 13
Saul, 35
Schiller, Johann Christoph Friedrich von, 4
Scott, Sir Walter, 3, 54
Shakespeare, William, 17; *Winter's Tale, The*, 102–3, 113
Simpson, Richard, 14, 15–17, 20
Speenhamland System, 50
Spinoza, Baruch: *Ethics*, 58
Stephen, Leslie, 14–15, 17–18, 53–54
Strauss, David Friedrich: *Life of Jesus*, 4, 15
Sturt, George: *Change in the Village*, 18

Taylor, Tom: *Our American Cousin*, 17
Teniers, David, 51–53
Tennyson, Alfred, Lord: "Aylmer's Field," 27; "Gardener's Daughter, The," 2
Thackeray, W. M., 3, 12, 54; *Vanity Fair*, 81
Thompson, Flora: *Lark Rise*, 19
Times (London), 14
Times Literary Supplement, 17
Trollope, Anthony, 3
Tyndall, John, 4

Unitarianism, 34

Virgil, 38

Wagner, Richard, 4
Warden, A. J.: *Linen Trade, The*, 19
Westminster Review, 4, 13, 51, 58, 112

Whale, J. S.: *Protestant Tradition,
The,* 36
Wilkie, David, 52
Williams, Raymond: *Country and
the City, The,* 19
Wordsworth, William: "Anecdote
for Fathers," 25; *Excursion,
The,* 112; "Immortality Ode,"
104; "Mad Mother, The,"
24–25; "Michael," 6, 23,
25–27, 104–5; "Old
Cumberland Beggar, The," 27;
Prelude, The, 27; "Ruined
Cottage, The," 27; "Thorn,
The," 24; "Tintern Abbey,"
104; (with S. T. Coleridge)
Lyrical Ballads, The, 23–27, 51
Woolf, Virginia, 17

The Author

Patrick Swinden is Senior Lecturer in English Language and Literature at the University of Manchester. He was educated at King James's Grammar School, Almondbury, and at the Universities of Hull and Cambridge. He was awarded the degree of Ph.D. after completing a dissertation on realism in the French and English novel.

Dr. Swinden has published review essays and articles on a variety of literary subjects in *The Times Educational Supplement*, *The Critical Quarterly*, and *Notes and Queries*, as well as in several scholarly symposia. He has edited collections of essays on George Eliot's *Middlemarch* and on Shelley's shorter poems and lyrics. His books include *Unofficial Selves: Character in the Novel from Dickens to the Present Day*; *Paul Scott: Images of India*; and *The English Novel of History and Society, 1940–1980*. At present he is working on a book about Kant's aesthetic and the theory of intention.